ERNEST G. MOORE

MEDITERRANEAN DIET COOKBOOK

Recipes & Tips For Healthy Eating

Copyright
© ERNEST G. MOORE

DISCLAIMER

Please note the information contain within this document is for educational and entertainment purpose only. All effort has been executed to present accurate, up to date, reliable, and complete information. No warranties of any kind are declared or implied. Readers acknowledge that the author is not engaged in the rendering of legal, financial, medical or professional advice.

The content within this book has been derived from various sources. Please consult a licensed professional before attempting any techniques outlined in this book. By reading this document the reader agrees that under no circumstances is the author responsible for any losses, direct or indirect, that are incurred as a result of the use of the information contained within this document, including, but not limited to, errors, omissions, or inaccuracies.

TABLE OF CONTENTS

WELCOME TO THE MEDITERRANEAN DIET COOKBOOK A DELECTABLE PATH TO A HEALTHIER YOU!

Have you ever imagined a way to eat that would please your taste buds in addition to being beneficial for your health? Greetings and welcome to the incredible Mediterranean diet trip!

This isn't some restrictive, deprivation-based fad diet. It's a way of life influenced by the customs of the nations around the stunning Mediterranean Sea. Imagine colorful Italy, sun-drenched Greece, and spice-laden Morocco—all nations where people have long recognized the link between a healthy lifestyle and excellent cuisine.

There is no need to watch calories or exclude certain food categories from the Mediterranean diet. The key is to embrace whole, fresh foods and allow them to take center stage. Imagine bowls brimming with in-season fruits and veggies, big olives dripping with olive oil, robust healthy grains, and fish and legumes that are high in protein. Your plate is a symphony of tastes, textures, and colors that all come together to entice your taste buds and fuel your body.

But there's still more! The Mediterranean lifestyle emphasizes a comprehensive approach to health rather than simply what's on your plate. It encourages sharing meals with loved ones, taking your time to enjoy them, and getting some exercise throughout the day.

The Mediterranean diet may serve as a guide for anybody seeking to increase their energy levels, enhance their heart health, or feel better overall. This book is your road map; it is filled with mouthwatering recipes, practical advice, and endless inspiration to help you set off on a life-changing adventure.

Are you prepared to give up processed meals and explore a world of vivid health and fresh flavors? One mouthwatering meal at a time, let's plunge in and experience the Mediterranean's sun-kissed coasts together!

WHY SHOULD YOU ADOPT A MEDITERRANEAN DIET?

THIS IS YOUR PASS TO A HEALTHIER, TASTIER YOU!

Imagine yourself relaxing on a patio with a view of the glistening Mediterranean Sea and the aroma of fresh herbs and olive orchards carried by a light wind. A table full of bright delicacies awaits you: a tray of grilled fish dripping with flavorful olive oil, a vivid salad full of juicy tomatoes and crisp cucumbers, and warm, crusty bread that's ideal for dipping into creamy hummus. This is a window into the core of the Mediterranean diet, not merely a dream holiday!

What, then, is this seemingly perfect dietary regimen? The Mediterranean diet is a concept that draws inspiration from the traditional cuisines of the nations that border the Mediterranean Sea, rather than a strict set of rules. Think of Italy with its fresh pasta and slow-cooked tomato sauces, Greece with its colorful salads and tangy feta cheese, and Spain with its seafood paella and tasty tapas. These cultures have a profound appreciation for seasonal, fresh foods as well as a concentration on complete grains, healthy fats, and an abundance of veggies.

However, why go with a Mediterranean diet? The truth is that it's not just about having great food—though, let's be honest; it's a pretty major bonus! There is several possible health advantages to this eating style may have several health benefits, including:

- *A diet for a happy heart:* Heart health benefits greatly from the Mediterranean diet. Focusing on heart-healthy fats, such as fish high in Omega-3 fatty acids and olive oil, may help you maintain your heart health and reduce harmful cholesterol.
- *Bid adieu to weight struggles:* Welcome to a satiated and invigorated state! Whole grains, legumes, and plenty of fiber are encouraged in the Mediterranean diet, which helps you naturally regulate your weight and feel fuller for longer.

- *Controlling the sugar demon:* This diet substitutes fruits' natural sweetness with manufactured sugars and refined carbs. This may assist in controlling blood sugar levels and provide you with stability throughout the day.
- *Boost brainpower:* The benefits of the Mediterranean diet extend beyond weight loss—it also has positive psychological effects! According to studies, it could help maintain your memory and cognitive performance for years to come.
- *A sensory extravaganza:* It's true that eating healthily shouldn't be monotonous or uninteresting! The Mediterranean diet celebrates vibrant, fresh foods. Making healthy choices is really delightful, since every meal is a sensory experience.

The finest aspect? There is no sense of deprivation or missing out on things while following a Mediterranean diet. It's about exploring a whole new world of scrumptious and healthy options. It's all about using seasonal produce, bold tastes, and a diet that feeds both your body and spirit. So give up on restrictive programs and fad diets and come along with us on a delectable journey to a happier, healthier you!

THE MEDITERRANEAN DIET'S BENEFITS: REVEALING SUNSHINE ON YOUR PLATE

Imagine enjoying delectable and filling meals while feeling energized all day long, your heart robust and healthy, and your mind clear and concentrated. It sounds really wonderful, doesn't it? That is how the Mediterranean diet works its magic!

This is not only about eating delicious food—though, let's be honest, it's a great benefit—this eating style was inspired by the sun-drenched nations that surround the Mediterranean Sea. Numerous possible health advantages of the Mediterranean diet might completely change your overall well-being.

- **A Heartfelt Feast:** Consider your heart to be a life-giving force. In the Mediterranean diet, it is given the respect it deserves! This diet may help decrease bad cholesterol, reduce inflammation in your arteries, and keep your heart happy and healthy because it places a strong emphasis on heart-healthy fats like olive oil, which is high in antioxidants, and seafood that is bursting with Omega-3 fatty acids. It is similar to using the best lubricants to give your internal engine a tune-up!

- **Easy weight management:** It's not enjoyable to feel lethargic and burdened by bad habits; let's face it. There is an easy way to get a healthy weight with the Mediterranean diet. Rich in fiber-rich whole grains, lentils, and an abundance of veggies, it helps you naturally regulate your weight by preventing cravings and prolonging feelings of fullness. Consider replacing processed, high-calorie snacks with substantial, nutrient-dense meals that satisfy you without feeling deprived.

- **Controlling the Glucose Rollercoaster:** Are you experiencing a sudden drop in energy after a sweet treat? Those fluctuations in blood sugar may be lessened with a Mediterranean diet. Eschewing refined carbs and processed sweets in favor of the naturally sweet flavors found in fruits and healthy grains helps control blood sugar levels, leaving you feeling steady and invigorated all day. Imagine being always focused and prepared to take on any task, without the afternoon slump!

- **Increasing Intelligence:** The Mediterranean diet is a hidden weapon that might help you maintain mental clarity! According to studies, consuming a diet high in antioxidants and good fats may enhance memory and cognitive performance. Consider it brain fuel that keeps your gray matter healthy and functioning at its maximum capacity. Goodbye to mental fog, and welcome to mental clarity!

- **A Joyful Celebration of Taste and Health:** The greatest advantage is, of course, the simple delight of eating wonderful, filling meals! The Mediterranean diet is about enjoying fresh, seasonal products and turning them into delicious meals, not about boring constraints. Every meal, from luscious grilled fish drenched in olive oil to herb-infused roasted veggies, is a celebration of vivid tastes and textures. It's an eating style that fills you up from the inside out, leaving you feeling not just well but really content.

The Mediterranean diet is a lifestyle change that provides several advantages for both your physical and mental health. It's not simply a diet. It's about enjoying the delightful path of healthy living, feeling your best, and having the energy to pursue your aspirations. Are you prepared to welcome the sunlight into your life and open the door to a happier and healthier you?

STARTING YOUR MEDITERRANEAN JOURNEY: AN EASY FIRST STEP

You want to know more about the amazing health advantages of the Mediterranean diet, right? You have every right to be curious! Eating this way is about adopting a tasty and enjoyable approach to a healthy you, not simply about feeling good.

But how even do you start? You are not alone on this adventure, so don't worry! To help you get started on your Mediterranean journey, *consider the following helpful advice:*

- "Little Steps Achieve Big Results" Implementing small, lifestyle-appropriate modifications is the secret to success. Don't attempt to make major changes all at once. To increase the amount of vegetables in your meals, start with a side salad for lunch or roast some vibrant vegetables for supper.
- Pick up necessities for the pantry: Consider your cupboard to be a treasure trove of Mediterranean goods! Load up on nutritious mainstays such as brown rice, lentils, beans, olive oil, and whole grain pasta. Remember to add flavor with dried herbs like basil and oregano, high-quality balsamic vinegar, and a variety of nuts and seeds.
- Get along with Seasonal and Fresh: The foundation and essence of the Mediterranean diet are fresh, in-season vegetables.

Visit your neighborhood grocery store or farmer's market to discover the colorful abundance of the current season. Imagine crisp winter greens, juicy summer tomatoes, and all the delectable alternatives in between.

- Appreciate Olive Oil's Power: This golden drink is an essential part of the Mediterranean diet. Give up butter and bad fats and embrace olive oil's heart-healthy benefits. It can be used to dip crusty bread, pour over salads, or cook.

- Seafood Superstar: Instead of red meat, treat yourself to the sea's marvels! Try to include fish and seafood in two or more of your meals each week. Full of vital minerals and rich in Omega-3 fatty acids, tuna, mussels, and salmon are all great options.

- Herbs and Spices: Don't Be Afraid: The secret components that turn ordinary meals into taste explosions are fresh herbs and spices. Try adding garlic, thyme, rosemary, oregano, and chili flakes to your food to give it a Mediterranean flavor.

- Reevaluate your sources of protein: Plant-based protein intake is encouraged to increase in the Mediterranean diet. Tofu, beans, lentils, and chickpeas are all great substitutes for meat that are filling.

- Turn water into your greatest ally: Drinking enough water is essential for good health in general, and the Mediterranean diet is no different. Make water your preferred beverage and avoid sugar-filled beverages. For a cool variation, add some fruit or cucumber slices to it.

- Mediterranean Style Sweet Treats: You don't have to completely give up dessert, so don't worry! The Mediterranean diet promotes enjoying fruits' inherent sweetness as well as rare sweets like dark chocolate or baklava. Ah, moderation is the key!

- Share with Joy, Cook with Love: Food is about celebration and connection, not simply about providing nourishment. Spend time in the kitchen, enjoy meals with those you love, and relish the moment. This careful eating technique is a fundamental component of the Mediterranean diet.

Recall that the Mediterranean diet is a process rather than a final goal. It's about having fun, trying out new cuisines, and choosing healthful options that work for your lifestyle. You'll be well on your way to enjoying the many benefits of this tasty and fulfilling diet if you use these pointers as a guide. Thus, prepare for a delectable journey towards a healthy you by gathering Mediterranean treasures for your pantry and grabbing your imaginary passport!

ACCEPT PLENTY: APPETIZING MEALS TO ENJOY ON A MEDITERRANEAN DIET

The Mediterranean diet celebrates an abundance of flavorful and nourishing meals rather than advocating for restriction. The following is a list of the main components of this colorful diet:

HOLD YOUR ARMS OUT:

- *Veggies and Fruits:* These vibrant stars command attention! Arrange a rainbow of in-season vegetables on your platter, such as plump eggplant, juicy tomatoes, sweet bell peppers, and lush greens. Remember to use citrus fruits and berries for a hint of sweetness and high levels of antioxidants.
- *Complete Grains:* Replace processed carbs with whole grains' strength. Choose pasta, whole-wheat bread, brown rice, and quinoa. They provide you with steady energy and prolong the sensation of fullness.
- *Healthy Fats:* The unsung hero of the Mediterranean diet is olive oil. Use it to lend a hint of richness to foods, cook with them, and season salads. Avocados, nuts, and seeds are also great sources of heart-healthy fats that are essential for cell and heart health.
- *Verdures:* Chickpeas, lentils, and beans are nutrient-dense superfoods! They add flavor and versatility to your meals, and they are high in essential minerals, fiber, and protein. Enjoy them as a delectable main course or in salads, stews, and soups.

- *Crustaceans and Fish:* Consider the abundance found in the Mediterranean Sea! Try to include fish and seafood in two or more of your meals each week. Omega-3 fatty acids found in salmon, sardines, tuna, mussels, and shrimp make them all great options for heart and brain health.
- *Dairy (Partially):* Eat dairy items in moderation, such as cheese and yogurt. To enjoy a smaller serving, use cheeses with a stronger taste profile and yogurt that is low-fat or fat-free.
- *Spices and Herbs:* Spices and fresh herbs provide a magical touch! Even the most basic meals benefit from their richness and depth of taste. To release your inner Mediterranean chef, discover the world of paprika, garlic, chili flakes, basil, rosemary, and thyme.

REDUCE OR STAY AWAY:

- *Swed Meat:* The Mediterranean diet recommends decreasing red meat intake, although it is not completely prohibited. Choose lean cuts and eat them sparingly—maybe once or twice a week.
- *Processed Meats:* High in harmful fats and salt, processed meats include hot dogs, bacon, and sausages. Avoiding them entirely or just occasionally enjoying them is advised.
- *Grains Refined:* The fiber and minerals are removed from white bread, spaghetti, and sugary cereals. To improve blood sugar regulation and provide longer-lasting energy, swap them out for whole-grain alternatives.
- *Added Sugars:* Give up soda, sugary drinks, and processed sweets. Choose naturally sweet fruits and sometimes indulge in sweets like baklava or dark chocolate, but always remember that moderation is the key!
- *Disgusting Fats:* Reduce your intake of processed snacks, fried meals, and fatty meat portions that include saturated and Trans fats. They may exacerbate heart disease and other health problems.
- *Keep in mind:* This is not a strict code of conduct. It serves as a guide to assist you in making wise decisions and adopting a diet that feeds both your body and spirit. Enjoy the path to a better you while concentrating on the plethora of tasty and healthy alternatives that the Mediterranean diet has to offer!

CHAPTER 1

BREAK-FAST

1 MEDITERRANEAN VEGETABLE FRITTATA

Prep Time: 15 minutes Cooking Time: 25 minutes Total Time: 40 minutes Servings: 4

Ingredients

- 6 big eggs 1/4 cup milk (or unsweetened almond milk)
- 1 tablespoon extra virgin olive oil
- 1 onion, diced 1 red bell pepper, diced
- 1 zucchini, diced
- 1 cup cherry tomatoes, halved
- 1/2 cup crumbled feta cheese
- 2 tablespoons chopped fresh parsley
- Salt and pepper to taste.

Nutritional value:
- Calories: 180 kcal, Fat: 10g
- Carbohydrates: 7g , Protein: 14g

Directions

1. Preheat the oven to 350°F (175°C).

2. In a large mixing basin, whisk together the eggs and milk until thoroughly blended. Season with salt and pepper, to taste.

3. Heat the olive oil in an oven-safe skillet over medium heat. Add the chopped onion and heat until softened, approximately 3–4 minutes.

4. In a skillet, add the diced red bell pepper and diced zucchini. Cook, stirring occasionally, for another 3–4 minutes until the veggies are soft.

5. Pour the whisked eggs over the sautéed veggies in the pan, ensuring they are equally distributed.

6. Arrange the halved cherry tomatoes on top of the egg mixture in the skillet.

7. Sprinkle the crumbled feta cheese on top of the frittata.

8. Transfer the pan to the preheated oven and bake for 20–25 minutes, or until the frittata is set in the middle and the sides are golden brown.

9. Once done, take the frittata from the oven and allow it to cool for a few minutes.

10. Garnish with chopped fresh parsley before slicing and serving.

QUICK TIPS

Feel free to personalize this frittata by adding additional Mediterranean veggies such as spinach, mushrooms, or olives. Leftover frittatas may be kept in an airtight jar in the refrigerator for up to 2 days. It's great served cold or warmed.

14

2 GREEK YOGURT PARFAIT WITH FRESH FRUIT & HONEY

Prep Time: 10 minutes Cooking Time: 0 minutes Total Time: 10 minutesServings: 2

Ingredients

- 1 cup Greek yogurt (plain or vanilla)
- 1 cup mixed fresh berries (such as strawberries, blueberries, and raspberries)
- 1/4 cup granola; 2 teaspoons honey
- 1 tablespoon chopped nuts (such as almonds or walnuts)

Nutritional value:
- Calories: 220 kcal
- Fat: 3g
- Carbohydrates: 40g
- Protein: 15g

Directions

1. In two serving glasses or bowls, layer the Greek yogurt, mixed fresh berries, and granola.
2. Drizzle honey on top of each parfait.
3. Sprinkle chopped nuts over the top for extra crunch and taste.
4. Serve the Greek yogurt parfait immediately for a refreshing and healthy breakfast alternative.

QUICK TIPS

You may modify this parfait by adding your favorite fruits, such as sliced bananas, chopped mango, or kiwi. If you like a sweeter parfait, you may use flavored Greek yogurt or add a touch of extra honey. Feel free to be creative with the toppings! You may add shredded coconut, chia seeds, or a sprinkling of cinnamon for added taste and texture.

3 MEDITERRANEAN AVOCADO TOAST

Prep Time: 10 minutes Cooking Time: 5 minutes Total Time: 15 minutes Servings: 2

Ingredients

- 2 slices of whole-grain bread and 1 ripe avocado
- 1 tablespoon of lemon juice
- Salt and pepper to taste; 1 small tomato, sliced
- 2 tablespoons crumbled feta cheese
- 1 tablespoon chopped fresh parsley or basil
- Optional toppings: sliced cucumber, red onion, olives, or a splash of balsamic glaze.

Nutritional value:
- Calories: 250 kcal
- Fat: 18g
- Carbohydrates: 19g
- Protein: 6g

Directions

1. Toast the pieces of whole-grain bread till golden brown and crispy.
2. While the bread is toasting, halves the avocado, removes the pit, and spoons the flesh into a small dish.
3. Mash the avocado with a fork until smooth and creamy. Stir in the lemon juice, and season to taste with salt and pepper.
4. Spread the mashed avocado equally across the toasted bread pieces.

5. Top each avocado toast with sliced tomato, crumbled feta cheese, and chopped fresh parsley or basil.
6. Add any extra toppings of your choosing, such as sliced cucumber, red onion, or olives.
7. Serve the Mediterranean avocado toast immediately for a pleasant and healthy breakfast.

QUICK TIPS

Experiment with various bread kinds, such as whole wheat, sourdough, or multigrain, for extra taste and texture. You may personalize your avocado toast with additional toppings such as poached eggs, smoked salmon, or arugula for more protein and taste

4 MEDITERRANEAN OMELETTE WITH SPINACH, FETA, & TOMATOES

Prep Time: 10 minutes Cooking Time: 10 minutes Total Time: 20 minutes Servings: 2

Ingredients

- 4 big eggs
- 1 tablespoon extra-virgin olive oil; 1 cup fresh spinach leaves
- 1 small tomato, diced 1/4 cup crumbled feta cheese
- Salt and pepper to taste; optional garnish: chopped fresh parsley or basil

Nutritional value:
- Calories: 220 kcal
- Fat: 15g
- Carbohydrates: 6g
- Protein: 14g

Directions

1. In a medium mixing basin, whisk together the eggs until fully beaten. Season with salt and pepper, to taste.
2. Heat the olive oil in a non-stick skillet over medium heat.
3. Add the fresh spinach leaves to the pan and heat until wilted, approximately 1-2 minutes.
4. Pour the beaten eggs into the pan, turning to thoroughly spread the spinach.
5. Cook the omelette for 2-3 minutes, or until the edges begin to firm.
6. Sprinkle the chopped tomato and crumbled feta cheese equally over one side of the omelette.
7. Carefully fold the second half of the omelette over the filling, forming a half-moon shape.
8. Cook for a further 2-3 minutes, or until the omelette is cooked through and the cheese is melted.
9. Slide the omelette onto a platter and garnish with chopped fresh parsley or basil, if preferred.
10. Serve the Mediterranean omelette hot, either on its own or with a side of whole grain bread or mixed greens.

QUICK TIPS

Feel free to personalize your omelette with extra ingredients such as chopped olives, diced bell peppers, or sautéed mushrooms.
For a dairy-free version, you may swap the feta cheese with dairy-free cheese or eliminate it completely.

5 MEDITERRANEAN BREAKFAST BOWL WITH QUINOA, HUMMUS, & VEGETABLES

Prep Time: 10 minutes Cooking Time: 15 minutes Total Time: 25 minutes Servings: 2

Ingredients

- 1/2 cup quinoa, rinsed 1 cup of water 1 cup mixed fresh veggies (such as cherry tomatoes, cucumber, bell pepper, and radishes), diced
- 1/2 cup hummus
- 2 tablespoons chopped fresh parsley; 1 tablespoon extra virgin olive oil; 1 tablespoon lemon juice
- Salt and pepper to taste Optional toppings: sliced olives, crumbled feta cheese, chopped almonds, or a drizzle of tahini sauce.

Nutritional value:
- Calories: 300 kcal
- Fat: 12g
- Carbohydrates: 40g
- Protein: 10g

Directions

1. In a small saucepan, mix the washed quinoa and water. Bring to a boil over medium heat, then decrease heat to low, cover, and simmer for 12–15 minutes, or until the quinoa is cooked and the water is absorbed. Remove from heat and let it settle, covered, for 5 minutes. Use a fork to fluff.

2. In a medium mixing bowl, combine the diced fresh veggies with chopped fresh parsley, extra virgin olive oil, lemon juice, salt, and pepper. Toss until evenly coated.

3. Divide the cooked quinoa into two serving dishes.

4. Top each dish of quinoa with a large tablespoon of hummus and the mixed veggie salad.

5. Add any extra toppings of your choosing, such as sliced olives, crumbled feta cheese, chopped almonds, or a drizzle of tahini sauce.

6. Serve the Mediterranean breakfast bowls immediately for a pleasant and nutrient-rich start to your day.

QUICK TIPS

You may personalize your breakfast bowl with additional ingredients such as roasted chickpeas, grilled chicken, or avocado slices for more protein and taste.
Make sure to rinse the quinoa completely before cooking to eliminate any bitterness from the outer covering.

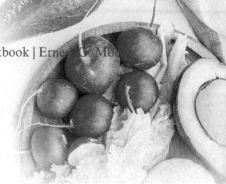

6 MEDITERRANEAN SHAKSHUKA

Prep Time: 10 minutes Cooking Time: 20 minutes Total Time: 30 minutes Servings: 2

Ingredients

- 4 big eggs 1 tablespoon of olive oil 1 onion, chopped; 2 cloves garlic, minced 1 red bell pepper, diced
- 1 yellow bell pepper, chopped
- 1 can (14 oz) chopped tomatoes
- 2 tablespoons of tomato paste
- 1 teaspoon ground cumin, 1 teaspoon paprika
- 1/2 teaspoon ground cayenne pepper (optional, for heat)
- Salt and pepper to taste; 2 tablespoons chopped fresh parsley or cilantro
- Crumbled feta cheese for garnish (optional)

Nutritional value:
- Calories: 250 kcal
- Fat: 15g
- Carbohydrates: 18g
- Protein: 12g

Directions

1. Heat olive oil in a large pan over medium heat. Add chopped onion and sauté until translucent, approximately 5 minutes.

2. Add minced garlic and diced bell peppers to the skillet. Cook for another 3–4 minutes until the peppers are softened.

3. Stir in chopped tomatoes, tomato paste, ground cumin, paprika, and ground cayenne pepper (if using). Season with salt and pepper, to taste.

4. Simmer the tomato mixture for 5-7 minutes until it thickens slightly.

5. Using a spoon, make tiny wells in the tomato mixture and break the eggs into the wells.

6. Cover the pan and let the eggs simmer for 5-7 minutes, or until the egg whites are set but the yolks are still runny.

7. Once the eggs are cooked to your liking, sprinkle chopped fresh parsley or cilantro on top.

8. Serve the Mediterranean shakshuka hot, sprinkled with crumbled feta cheese if preferred. Serve with toasted bread or pita for dipping.

QUICK TIPS

Customize your shakshuka with extra ingredients like spinach, olives, or crumbled sausage for increased taste and diversity.
Adjust the amount of spiciness by adding more or less ground cayenne pepper according to your desire.

7 MEDITERRANEAN BREAKFAST WRAP

Prep Time: 10 minutes Cooking Time: 5 minutes Total Time: 15 minutes Servings: 2

Ingredients

- 2 big whole wheat tortillas; 4 large eggs
- 1 tablespoon of olive oil
- 1/2 cup baby spinach leaves
- 1/2 cup chopped tomatoes
- 1/4 cup sliced black olives
- 1/4 cup crumbled feta cheese
- Salt and pepper to taste Optional toppings: sliced avocado, chopped fresh parsley, or basil.

Nutritional value:
- Calories: 320 kcal
- Fat: 18g
- Carbohydrates: 28g
- Protein: 12g

Directions

1. Heat olive oil in a non-stick skillet over medium heat.

2. In a separate bowl, mix together the eggs until fully beaten. Season with salt and pepper, to taste.

3. Pour the beaten eggs into the pan and heat, stirring periodically, until scrambled and cooked through.

4. Warm the whole wheat tortillas in the microwave or on a griddle for a few seconds to make them flexible.

5. Divide the scrambled eggs equally between the two tortillas, spreading them out in the middle.

6. Top the scrambled eggs with baby spinach leaves, chopped tomatoes, sliced black olives, and crumbled feta cheese.

7. Add any extra toppings of your choosing, such as sliced avocado or chopped fresh herbs.

8. Roll up the tortillas firmly, tucking in the edges as you go, to make wraps.

9. Slice each wrap in half diagonally and serve immediately, or wrap in foil for a handy grab-and-go breakfast.

QUICK TIPS

Customize your breakfast wraps with extra contents such as cooked bacon, sliced bell peppers, or hummus for increased taste and protein.
To create a vegetarian version, skip the eggs and add additional veggies such as grilled mushrooms or roasted red peppers.

8 MEDITERRANEAN BREAKFAST QUINOA BOWL

Prep Time: 10 minutes Cooking Time: 15 minutes Total Time: 25 minutes Servings: 2

Ingredients

- 1/2 cup quinoa, rinsed 1 cup water, 1 tablespoon olive oil
- 1/2 red onion, diced
- 1 clove garlic, minced
- 1/2 red bell pepper, chopped
- 1/2 yellow bell pepper, chopped
- 1/2 zucchini, diced
- 1 cup cherry tomatoes, halved
- 2 tablespoons minced fresh parsley 1 tablespoon of lemon juice
- Salt and pepper to taste Optional toppings: sliced avocado, crumbled feta cheese, poached egg

Nutritional value:
- Calories: 280 kcal
- Fat: 10g
- Carbohydrates: 38g
- Protein: 10g

Directions

1. In a small saucepan, mix the washed quinoa and water. Bring to a boil over medium heat, then decrease heat to low, cover, and simmer for 12–15 minutes, or until the quinoa is cooked and the water is absorbed. Remove from heat and let it settle, covered, for 5 minutes. Use a fork to fluff.

2. While the quinoa is cooking, heat olive oil in a pan over medium heat. Add chopped red onion and minced garlic. Cook until softened, approximately 2–3 minutes.

3. Add diced red bell pepper, yellow bell pepper, and zucchini to the skillet. Cook until veggies are soft but still crisp, approximately 5-7 minutes.

4. Stir in cherry tomatoes, chopped fresh parsley, and lemon juice. Cook for a further 2–3 minutes.

5. To taste, season with salt and pepper.

6. Divide the cooked quinoa between two dishes. Top with cooked Mediterranean veggies.

7. Add extra toppings such as sliced avocado, crumbled feta cheese, or a poached egg if preferred.

8. Serve the Mediterranean breakfast quinoa bowls immediately, with a drizzle of olive oil or a squeeze of lemon juice if preferred.

QUICK TIPS

Feel free to personalize your morning quinoa bowls with your favorite Mediterranean veggies, such as eggplant, artichoke hearts, or spinach. You may cook a larger quantity of quinoa and keep the leftovers in the refrigerator for quick and simple breakfasts throughout the week.

9 GREEK YOGURT PANCAKES WITH HONEY AND BERRIES

Prep Time: 10 minutes Cooking Time: 10 minutes Total Time: 20 minutes Servings: 2 (makes roughly 6 pancakes)

Ingredients

- 1 cup all-purpose flour; 1 tablespoon granulated sugar; 1 teaspoon baking powder
- 1/2 teaspoon baking soda
- 1 teaspoon salt and 1 cup Greek yogurt
- Two big eggs
- 1 teaspoon vanilla extract; 2 tablespoons unsalted butter, melted
- Honey, for serving
- Fresh berries for serving

Nutritional value:
- Calories: 250 kcal
- Fat: 6g
- Carbohydrates: 40g
- Protein: 10g

Directions

1. In a large mixing basin, whisk together the flour, sugar, baking powder, baking soda, and salt.

2. In a separate dish, mix together the Greek yogurt, eggs, vanilla extract, and melted butter until smooth.

3. Pour the wet ingredients into the dry ingredients and whisk until just incorporated. Do not overmix; a few lumps are alright.

4. Heat a non-stick skillet or griddle over medium heat. Lightly grease with butter or cooking spray.

5. Pour approximately 1/4 cup of batter onto the griddle for each pancake. Cook until bubbles form on the top, then turn and cook until golden brown on the other side, approximately 2–3 minutes per side.

6. Repeat with the remaining batter, coating the skillet as required.

7. Serve the Greek yogurt pancakes warm, topped with a drizzle of honey and fresh berries.

QUICK TIPS

For more protein, you may swap half of the all-purpose flour with protein powder or almond flour. These pancakes are wonderful with a dollop of Greek yogurt on top, along with more honey and berries for a Mediterranean-inspired touch

10 MEDITERRANEAN BREAKFAST BURRITO

Prep Time: 10 minutes Cooking Time: 10 minutes Total Time: 20 minutes Servings: 2

Ingredients

- 4 big eggs 1 tablespoon of olive oil 1/2 red onion, sliced
- 1 clove garlic, minced
- 1/2 red bell pepper, chopped
- 1/2 yellow bell pepper, chopped
- 1/2 zucchini, diced
- 1/2 cup cherry tomatoes, halved
- 2 teaspoons chopped fresh parsley
- Salt and pepper to taste; 2 big whole wheat tortillas
- 1/4 cup hummus 1/4 cup crumbled feta cheese

Nutritional value:
- Calories: 320 kcal
- Fat: 15g
- Carbohydrates: 28g
- Protein: 18g

Directions

. In a separate bowl, mix together the eggs until fully beaten. Season with salt and pepper, to taste.

2. Heat olive oil in a skillet over medium heat. Add chopped red onion and minced garlic. Cook until softened, approximately 2–3 minutes.

3. Add diced red bell pepper, yellow bell pepper, and zucchini to the skillet. Cook until veggies are soft but still crisp, approximately 5-7 minutes.

4. Stir in cherry tomatoes and chopped fresh parsley. Cook for a further 2–3 minutes.

5. Pour the beaten eggs into the pan with the cooked veggies. Cook, tossing occasionally, until scrambled and cooked through.

6. Warm the whole wheat tortillas in the microwave or on a griddle for a few seconds to make them flexible.

7. Spread hummus equally over each tortilla.

8. Divide the scrambled egg and veggie mixture between the two tortillas. Sprinkle crumbled feta cheese on top.

9. Roll up the tortillas firmly, tucking in the edges as you go, to make burritos.

10. Slice each tortilla in half diagonally and serve immediately.

QUICK TIPS

Customize your morning burritos with extra ingredients such as sliced avocado, chopped fresh herbs, or a splash of spicy sauce.

These burritos may be wrapped in foil and refrigerated in the refrigerator for a simple grab-and-go breakfast alternative. Simply reheat in the microwave before serving.

23

CHAPTER
LUNCH

2

1 MEDITERRANEAN QUINOA SALAD

Prep Time: 15 minutes; Cooking Time: 15 minutes; Total Time: 30 minutes; Servings: 4

Ingredients

- 1 cup quinoa, rinsed;
- 2 cups water or vegetable broth;
- 1 cucumber, diced;
- 1 cup cherry tomatoes, halved;
- 1/2 cup Kalamata olives, pitted and sliced
- 1/4 cup red onion, coarsely chopped
- 1/4 cup fresh parsley, chopped
- 1/4 cup feta cheese, crumbled
- 2 tablespoons extra virgin olive oil;
- 2 teaspoons lemon juice
- Salt and pepper to taste.

Nutritional value:

- Calories: 320
- Total Fat: 12g
- Carbohydrates: 45g
- Protein: 10g

Directions

1. In a medium saucepan, bring the water or vegetable broth to a boil. Add quinoa, lower the heat to low, cover, and simmer for 15 minutes, or until the quinoa is soft and water is absorbed.

2. Fluff the quinoa with a fork and move it to a large mixing bowl. Let it cool for a few minutes.

3. Add cucumber, cherry tomatoes, olives, red onion, parsley, and feta cheese to the bowl with the quinoa.

4. In a small bowl, stir together olive oil, lemon juice, salt, and pepper. Pour over the salad and toss lightly to mix.

5. Serve immediately or refrigerate for later. Enjoy!

QUICK TIPS

You may modify this salad by adding additional Mediterranean foods like roasted red peppers, artichoke hearts, or grilled chicken for added protein.

2 GREEK CHICKPEA WRAPS

Prep Time: 10 minutes; Cooking Time: 0 minutes; Total Time: 10 minutes; Servings: 2

Ingredients

- 1 can (15 ounces) of chickpeas, drained and rinsed
- 1/4 cup Greek yogurt
- 1 tablespoon of lemon juice
- 1/2 teaspoon garlic powder
- 1/2 teaspoon dried oregano
- Salt and pepper to taste; 2 whole wheat tortillas
- 1 cup of baby spinach leaves
- 1/2 cup cucumber, thinly sliced; 1/2 cup cherry tomatoes, halved 1/4 cup crumbled feta cheese

Nutritional value:
- Calories: 380
- Total Fat: 14g
- Carbohydrates: 50g
- Protein: 15g

Directions

1. In a mixing bowl, mash the chickpeas with a fork until they are somewhat mashed but still chunky.

2. Add Greek yogurt, lemon juice, garlic powder, dried oregano, salt, and pepper to the chickpeas. Stir until completely blended.

3. Lay out the tortillas and divide the chickpea mixture equally between them, spreading it out in the middle of each tortilla.

4. Top each tortilla with baby spinach leaves, cucumber slices, cherry tomatoes, and crumbled feta cheese.

5. Roll up the tortillas firmly, tucking in the edges as you go.

6. Slice each wrap in half and serve immediately.

You may add a drizzle of tzatziki sauce or hummus to the wraps for added flavor. For a full Mediterranean-inspired supper, serve with a side of olives or fresh fruit.

3 MEDITERRANEAN CHICKPEA SALAD

Prep Time: 15 minutes Cooking Time: 0 minutes Total Time:15 minutes Servings: 4

Ingredients

- 2 cans (15 ounces each) of chickpeas, drained and rinsed
- 1 English cucumber, diced;
- 1 cup cherry tomatoes, halved;
- 1/2 red onion, finely chopped;
- ¼cup chopped fresh mint leaves;
- 1/4 cup chopped fresh parsley leaves;
- 1/4 cup crumbled feta cheese (optional)

LEMON-OLIVE DRESSING:
- *1/4 cup extra-virgin olive oil 2 teaspoons of fresh lemon juice*
- *1 clove garlic, minced*
- *1 teaspoon dried oregano*
- *To taste, add salt and pepper.*

Nutritional value:
- Calories: 280 kcal
- Fat: 10g
- Carbohydrates: 35g
- Fiber: 10g

Directions

1. In a large mixing bowl, add chickpeas, cucumber, cherry tomatoes, red onion, mint, and parsley.

2. In a separate bowl, mix together olive oil, lemon juice, minced garlic, dried oregano, salt, and pepper to create the dressing.

3. Pour the dressing over the salad and toss lightly to coat.

4. Sprinkle with crumbled feta cheese, if preferred.

5. Serve chilled or at room temperature.

QUICK TIPS

This salad may be prepared ahead and kept in the refrigerator for up to 3 days. Feel free to add extra ingredients such as chopped bell peppers, olives, or avocado.

4 MEDITERRANEAN 1 STUFFED BELL PEPPERS

Prep Time: 20 minutes Cooking Time: 35 minutes Total Time:55 minutes Servings: 4

Ingredients

- 4 large bell peppers, halved and seeds removed;
- 1 cup cooked quinoa;
- 1 can (15 ounces) chickpeas, drained and rinsed;
- 1 cup cherry tomatoes, halved
- 1/2 cup diced cucumber
- 1/4 cup chopped fresh parsley;
- 1/4 cup crumbled feta cheese;
- 2 tablespoons extra-virgin olive oil;
- 2 teaspoons fresh lemon juice
- 1 teaspoon dried oregano
- To taste, add salt and pepper.

Nutritional value:
- Calories: 320 kcal
- Fat: 12g
- Carbohydrates: 35g
- Fiber: 8g
- Protein: 18g

Directions

1. Preheat the oven to 375°F (190°C).

2. In a large mixing bowl, add cooked quinoa, chickpeas, cherry tomatoes, cucumber, parsley, feta cheese, olive oil, lemon juice, dried oregano, salt, and pepper.

3. Mix thoroughly until all components are uniformly incorporated.

4. Place bell pepper halves on a baking sheet, cut side up.

5. Stuff each bell pepper half with the quinoa mixture until it's full.

6. Cover the baking sheet with aluminum foil, and bake for 25 minutes.

7. Remove the foil and bake for a further 10 minutes, or until the peppers are soft and gently browned.

8. Serve hot, topped with additional chopped parsley if preferred.

You may personalize the filling by adding items like chopped spinach, sliced onions, or pine nuts. Leftover stuffed peppers may be kept in the refrigerator for up to 3 days and warmed in the oven or microwave before serving.

5 MEDITERRANEAN VEGGIE & HUMMUS WRAP

Prep Time: 10 minutes Cooking Time: 0 minutes Total Time: 10 minutes Servings: 2

Ingredients

- 2 healthy wheat wraps or tortillas
- 1/2 cup hummus;
- 1 cup baby spinach leaves;
- 1/2 cucumber, thinly sliced;
- 1/2 red bell pepper, thinly sliced;
- 1/4 cup sliced black olives
- 1/4 cup crumbled feta cheese Fresh parsley or basil leaves for garnish (optional)

Nutritional value:
- Calories: 280 kcal
- Fat: 10g
- Carbohydrates: 35g
- Fiber: 8g
- Protein: 10g

Directions

1. Lay out the wraps on a clean surface.
2. Spread a large quantity of hummus onto each wrap.
3. Arrange baby spinach leaves, cucumber slices, red bell pepper slices, black olives, and crumbled feta cheese equally over the hummus.

4. Roll up the wraps firmly, tucking in the sides as you go.
5. Slice the wraps in half and serve immediately, topped with fresh parsley or basil leaves if preferred.

QUICK TIPS

You may add grilled chicken pieces or falafel for added protein if desired.
Feel free to swap any of the veggies with your favorites, such as shredded carrots, roasted red peppers, or cherry tomatoes.

6 MEDITERRANEAN TUNA SALAD

Prep Time: 15 minutes Cooking Time: 0 minutes Total Time: 15 minutes Servings: 2

Ingredients

- 2 cans (5 ounces each) of tuna, drained
- 1/4 cup chopped red onion;
- 1/4 cup diced cucumber
- 1/4 cup diced cherry tomatoes
- 1/4 cup sliced black olives
- 2 tablespoons chopped fresh parsley;
- 2 tablespoons extra-virgin olive oil;
- 1 tablespoon fresh lemon juice
- Salt and pepper to taste; mix salad greens for serving.

Nutritional value:
- Calories: 320 kcal
- Fat: 15g
- Carbohydrates: 10g
- Fiber: 3g
- Protein: 35g

Directions

1. In a large mixing bowl, add drained tuna, diced red onion, diced cucumber, diced cherry tomatoes, sliced black olives, and chopped fresh parsley.
2. Drizzle extra-virgin olive oil and fresh lemon juice over the tuna mixture.
3. To taste, season with salt and pepper.

4. Toss gently until all ingredients are fully blended.
5. Serve the Mediterranean tuna salad over a bed of mixed salad leaves.

QUICK TIPS

You may add additional ingredients to the salad, such as sliced bell peppers, capers, or chopped avocado. This salad may be served on whole-grain bread or in lettuce wraps for a low-carb alternative.

7 MEDITERRANEAN QUINOA STUFFED PEPPERS

Prep Time: 20 minutes Cooking Time: 40 minutes Total Time: 1 hour Servings: 4

Ingredients

- 4 large bell peppers, halved and seeds removed.
- 1 cup quinoa, washed
- 2 cups vegetable broth;
- 1 can (15 ounces) chickpeas, drained and rinsed
- 1 cup diced tomatoes;
- 1/2 cup diced red onion;
- 1/4 cup chopped fresh parsley;
- 1/4 cup crumbled feta cheese;
- 2 tablespoons extra-virgin olive oil;
- 1 tablespoon balsamic vinegar; 1 teaspoon dried oregano
- To taste, add salt and pepper.

Nutritional value:
- Calories: 320 kcal
- Fat: 10g
- Carbohydrates: 45g
- Fiber: 9g
- Protein: 14g

Directions

1. Preheat the oven to 375°F (190°C).

2. In a medium saucepan, bring the vegetable broth to a boil. Add quinoa, reduce heat to low, cover, and simmer for 15-20 minutes, or until liquid is absorbed and quinoa is cooked. Remove it from heat and let it cool.

3. In a large mixing bowl, add cooked quinoa, chickpeas, diced tomatoes, red onion, parsley, and crumbled feta cheese.

4. In a small bowl, mix together extra-virgin olive oil, balsamic vinegar, dried oregano, salt, and pepper.

5. Pour the dressing over the quinoa mixture and toss lightly to coat.

6. Stuff the quinoa mixture into each bell pepper half until it is full.

7. Place the filled peppers on a baking dish, cut side up.

8. Cover the baking dish with aluminum foil and bake for 30 minutes.

9. Remove the foil and bake for a further 10 minutes, or until the peppers are soft and the filling is cooked through.

10. Serve hot, topped with additional chopped parsley if preferred.

QUICK TIPS

You may personalize the filling by adding items like chopped olives, artichoke hearts, or pine nuts. Leftover stuffed peppers may be kept in the refrigerator for up to 3 days and warmed in the oven or microwave before serving.

8 MEDITERRANEAN LENTIL SALAD

Prep Time: 15 minutes Cooking Time: 20 minutes Total Time: 35 minutes Servings:4

Ingredients

- 1 cup dry green lentils;
- 2 cups water 1 cucumber, diced;
- 1 cup cherry tomatoes, halved;
- 1/2 red onion, finely chopped;
- 1/4 cup chopped fresh parsley;
- 1/4 cup crumbled feta cheese;
- 2 tablespoons extra-virgin olive oil;
- 2 tablespoons red wine vinegar;
- 1 teaspoon dried oregano
- To taste, add salt and pepper

Nutritional value:
- Calories: 250 kcal
- Fat: 8g
- Carbohydrates: 35g
- Fiber: 12g
- Protein: 12g

Directions

1. Rinse the lentils under cold water and drain.
2. In a medium saucepan, add the lentils and water. Bring to a boil, then reduce the heat to low, cover, and simmer for 15-20 minutes, or until the lentils are soft but still retain their form. Drain any extra water and let the lentils cool.
3. In a large mixing bowl, add cooked lentils, cucumber, cherry tomatoes, red onion, parsley, and crumbled feta cheese.

4. In a small bowl, mix together extra-virgin olive oil, red wine vinegar, dried oregano, salt, and pepper.
5. Pour the dressing over the lentil mixture and toss lightly to coat.
6. Serve chilled or at room temperature.

You may add additional ingredients like chopped bell peppers, olives, or avocado. This salad may be prepared ahead and kept in the refrigerator for up to 3 days.

9 MEDITERRANEAN FALAFEL WRAP

Prep Time: 20 minutes (if using pre-made falafel) Cooking Time: 10 minutes Total Time:30 minutes
Servings: 2

Ingredients

- 4 falafel patties (store-bought or homemade)
- 2 whole wheat wraps or tortillas
- 1/2 cup hummus
- 1/2 cup shredded lettuce
- 1/2 cup diced tomatoes,
- 1/4 cup diced cucumber
- 1/4 cup diced red onion;
- 2 teaspoons minced fresh parsley;
- 2 tablespoons tzatziki sauce (optional)
- To taste, add salt and pepper.

Nutritional value:
- Calories: 350 kcal
- Fat: 12g
- Carbohydrates: 45g
- Fiber: 8g
- Protein: 15g

Directions

1. If using store-bought falafel, follow the package directions to cook them until they're crispy and cooked through. If using handmade falafel, fry or bake them according to your recipe's directions.
2. Warm the wraps or tortillas in a dry pan for a few seconds on each side until they're malleable.
3. Spread a layer of hummus onto each wrap.
4. Divide the shredded lettuce, diced tomatoes, diced cucumber, diced red onion, and chopped parsley equally between the wraps.

5. Place two falafel patties on each wrap.
6. Drizzle tzatziki sauce over the falafel, if desired.
7. Season to taste with salt and pepper.
8. Roll up the wraps securely, tucking in the sides as you go.
9. Slice the wraps in half and serve immediately.

QUICK TIPS

You may prepare your own falafel using chickpeas, herbs, and spices for a healthier choice. Add sliced avocado or olives for added flavor and nutrition.

10 MEDITERRANEAN COUSCOUS SALAD

Prep Time: 15 minutes Cooking Time: 10 minutes Total Time: 25 minutes Servings: 4

Ingredients

- 1 cup couscous;
- 1 1/2 cups veggie broth or water
- 1/4 cup extra-virgin olive oil;
- 2 teaspoons lemon juice
- 1 clove garlic, minced
- 1 teaspoon ground cumin;
- 1/2 teaspoon paprika
- Salt and pepper to taste;
- 1 cup diced cucumber
- 1 cup cherry tomatoes, halved
- 1/2 cup minced fresh parsley
- 1/4 cup sliced black olives
- 1/4 cup crumbled feta cheese (optional)

Nutritional value:
- Calories: 280 kcal
- Fat: 8g
- Carbohydrates: 45g
- Fiber: 6g
- Protein: 8g

Directions

1. In a medium saucepan, bring vegetable broth or water to a boil. Stir in couscous, cover, and remove from heat. Let it set for 5 minutes, then fluff with a fork and let it cool.
2. In a separate bowl, mix together olive oil, lemon juice, minced garlic, ground cumin, paprika, salt, and pepper to create the dressing.
3. In a large mixing bowl, add cooled couscous, diced cucumber, split cherry tomatoes, chopped fresh parsley, sliced black olives, and crumbled feta cheese.
4. Pour the dressing over the couscous mixture and toss lightly to coat
5. Serve chilled or at room temperature.

You may add additional ingredients like chopped bell peppers, red onion, or chickpeas for more flavor and texture.
This salad makes a terrific side dish or a light main entrée for lunch.

CHAPTER
DINNER
3

1 MEDITERRANEAN LEMON HERB GRILLED CHICKEN

Prep Time: 15 minutes Marinating Time: 30 minutes Cooking Time: 15 minutes Total Time: 1 hour
Servings: 4

Ingredients

- 4 boneless, skinless chicken breasts
- 1/4 cup extra-virgin olive oil;
- 2 teaspoons fresh lemon juice
- 2 cloves garlic, minced
- 1 teaspoon dried oregano;
- 1 teaspoon dry thyme;
- 1 teaspoon dried rosemary
- Salt and pepper to taste;
- lemon wedges for serving; chopped fresh parsley for garnish

Nutritional value:

- Calories: 280 kcal
- Fat: 12g
- Carbohydrates: 5g
- Fiber: 1g
- Protein: 35g

Directions

1. In a small bowl, mix together extra-virgin olive oil, fresh lemon juice, minced garlic, dried oregano, dried thyme, dried rosemary, salt, and pepper to form the marinade.

2. Place chicken breasts in a resealable plastic bag or shallow dish. Pour the marinade over the chicken, ensuring that each piece is covered equally. Seal the bag or cover the dish and refrigerate for at least 30 minutes, or up to 4 hours.

3. Preheat the grill to medium-high heat.

4. Remove the chicken from the marinade and discard any extra marinade.

5. Grill chicken breasts for 6–8 minutes on each side, or until they are cooked through and have grill marks.

6. Remove them from the grill and let them rest for a few minutes.

7. Serve hot, topped with chopped fresh parsley and lemon wedges on the side.

QUICK TIPS

Serve grilled chicken with a side of quinoa, couscous, or roasted veggies for a full dinner.
Make enough marinade to serve as a sauce for pouring over the cooked chicken.

2 MEDITERRANEAN BAKED SALMON WITH HERB CRUST

Prep Time: 15 minutes Marinating Time: 30 minutes Cooking Time: 15 minutes Total Time: 1 hour
Servings: 4

Ingredients

- 4 salmon fillets (approximately 6 ounces each), skin-on or skinless
- 1/4 cup extra-virgin olive oil
- 2 teaspoons of fresh lemon juice
- 2 cloves garlic, minced
- 1 tablespoon chopped fresh parsley;
- 1 tablespoon chopped fresh dill;
- 1 tablespoon chopped fresh basil
- 1/2 cup breadcrumbs (use whole wheat breadcrumbs for a healthier choice)
- Salt and pepper to taste; lemon wedges for serving

Nutritional value:

- Calories: 300 kcal
- Fat: 15g
- Carbohydrates: 3g
- Fiber: 1g
- Protein: 35g

Directions

1. In a small bowl, mix together extra-virgin olive oil, fresh lemon juice, minced garlic, chopped fresh parsley, chopped fresh dill, chopped fresh basil, salt, and pepper to form the marinade.

2. Place the salmon fillets in a shallow dish and pour the marinade over them, ensuring that each fillet is covered equally. Cover the dish and refrigerate for at least 30 minutes, or up to 4 hours.

3. Preheat the oven to 400°F (200°C). Line a baking sheet with parchment paper or gently coat it with olive oil.

4. In another small dish, combine breadcrumbs with a drizzle of olive oil and stir until the breadcrumbs are evenly coated.

5. Remove the salmon fillets from the marinade and set them on the prepared baking sheet.

6. Press the breadcrumb mixture onto the top of each salmon fillet to make a crust.

7. Bake in the preheated oven for 12–15 minutes, or until the salmon is cooked through and the crust is golden brown.

8. Remove from the oven and allow the salmon to rest for a few minutes before serving.

9. Serve hot, garnished with lemon slices on the side.

QUICK TIPS

Serve baked salmon with a side of roasted veggies or a mixed green salad dressed with a lemon vinaigrette. Adjust the baking time based on the thickness of your salmon fillets to ensure they are cooked through yet remain moist.

3 MEDITERRANEAN VEGETABLE PAELLA

Prep Time: 15 minutes Cooking Time: 40 minutes Total Time: 55 minutes Servings: 4

Ingredients

- 1 tablespoon olive oil; 1 onion, chopped
- 2 cloves garlic, minced
- 1 red bell pepper, sliced 1 yellow bell pepper, sliced
- 1 zucchini, diced
- 1 cup cherry tomatoes, halved
- 1 cup Arborio rice; 2 cups vegetable broth; 1 teaspoon smoked paprika
- 1 teaspoon dried thyme; salt and pepper to taste; 1/4 cup chopped fresh parsley
- Lemon wedges for serving

Nutritional value:

- Calories: 280 kcal
- Fat: 8g
- Carbohydrates: 45g
- Fiber: 8g
- Protein: 10g

Directions

1. Heat olive oil in a large skillet or paella pan over medium heat. Add chopped onion and minced garlic, and sauté until softened, approximately 2–3 minutes.

2. Add sliced red bell pepper, sliced yellow bell pepper, chopped zucchini, and half cherry tomatoes to the pan. Cook for another 5 minutes, stirring periodically.

3. Stir in Arborio rice, smoked paprika, dried thyme, salt, and pepper. Cook for 1-2 minutes to toast the rice and seasonings.

4. Pour vegetable broth into the pan and bring to a boil. Reduce heat to low, cover, and simmer for 20–25 minutes, or until the rice is cooked and most of the liquid is absorbed.

5. Remove from the heat and let the paella rest, covered, for 5 minutes.

6. Sprinkle chopped fresh parsley over the paella before serving.

7. Serve hot, with lemon wedges on the side for squeezing over the paella.

You may add different veggies, such as artichoke hearts, green beans, or peas, to personalize your paella. For a protein boost, add cooked shrimp, chicken, or tofu.

4 MEDITERRANEAN STUFFED BELL PEPPERS

Prep Time: 20 minutes Cooking Time: 40 minutes Total Time: 1 hour Servings: 4

Ingredients

- 4 large bell peppers, halved and seeds removed;
- 1 cup cooked quinoa;
- 1 can (15 ounces) chickpeas, drained and rinsed;
- 1 cup diced tomatoes;
- 1/2 cup diced red onion;
- 1/4 cup chopped fresh parsley;
- 1/4 cup crumbled feta cheese;
- 2 tablespoons extra-virgin olive oil;
- 2 tablespoons red wine vinegar;
- 1 teaspoon dried oregano
- To taste, add salt and pepper.

Nutritional value:
- Calories: 250 kcal
- Fat: 8g
- Carbohydrates: 35g
- Fiber: 8g
- Protein: 12g

Directions

1. Preheat the oven to 375°F (190°C).

2. In a large mixing bowl, add cooked quinoa, chickpeas, diced tomatoes, red onion, parsley, and crumbled feta cheese.

3. In a separate bowl, mix together extra-virgin olive oil, red wine vinegar, dried oregano, salt, and pepper to create the dressing.

4. Pour the dressing over the quinoa mixture and toss lightly to coat.

5. Stuff each bell pepper half with the quinoa mixture until it's full.

6. Place the filled peppers on a baking tray, cut side up.

7. Cover the baking dish with aluminum foil and bake for 30 minutes.

8. Remove the cover and bake for a further 10 minutes, or until the peppers are soft and the filling is cooked through.

9. Serve hot, garnished with additional chopped parsley if preferred.

QUICK TIPS

You may personalize the filling by adding items like chopped olives, artichoke hearts, or pine nuts. Leftover stuffed peppers may be kept in the refrigerator for up to 3 days and warmed in the oven or microwave before serving.

5 MEDITERRANEAN SHRIMP AND VEGETABLE SKEWERS

Prep Time: 20 minutes Marinating Time: 30 minutes Cooking Time: 10 minutes Total Time: 1 hour
Servings: 4

Ingredients

- 1 pound of big shrimp, peeled and deveined;
- 1 zucchini, chopped into rounds
- 1 yellow bell pepper, cut into pieces
- 1 red onion, cut into bits
- 1 pint of cherry tomatoes
- 1/4 cup extra-virgin olive oil
- 2 teaspoons of fresh lemon juice
- 2 cloves garlic, minced
- 1 teaspoon dried oregano
- Salt and pepper to taste;
- wooden or metal skewers

Nutritional value:
- Calories: 220 kcal
- Fat: 8g
- Carbohydrates: 10g
- Fiber: 3g
- Protein: 25g

Directions

1. If using wooden skewers, soak them in water for at least 30 minutes to avoid scorching.

2. In a small bowl, mix together extra-virgin olive oil, fresh lemon juice, minced garlic, dried oregano, salt, and pepper to form the marinade.

3. Place shrimp and cut veggies in a large mixing basin. Pour the marinade over them and toss lightly to coat. Let them marinade in the refrigerator for at least 30 minutes, or up to 2 hours.

4. Preheat the grill to medium-high heat.

5. Thread shrimp and veggies onto skewers, rotating between them.

6. Grill skewers for 3–4 minutes on each side, or until shrimp are pink and veggies are cooked and faintly browned.

7. Remove from the grill and serve hot.

QUICK TIPS

You may change the veggie choices depending on your tastes. Mushrooms, cherry tomatoes, and bell peppers work great on skewers.
Serve the skewers with a serving of whole-grain couscous or a mixed green salad.

6 MEDITERRANEAN EGGPLANT PARMESAN

Prep Time: 30 minutes Cooking Time: 45 minutes Total Time: 1 hour 15 minutes Servings: 4

Ingredients

- 2 big eggplants, cut into 1/4-inch rounds
- 2 cups marinara sauce
- 1 cup breadcrumbs (use whole wheat breadcrumbs for a healthier choice)
- 1/2 cup grated Parmesan cheese
- 2 eggs, beaten
- 1/4 cup chopped fresh basil;
- 1/4 cup chopped fresh parsley;
- salt and pepper to taste; olive oil for frying

Nutritional value:
- Calories: 280 kcal
- Fat: 15g
- Carbohydrates: 20g
- Fiber: 6g
- Protein: 15g

Directions

1. Preheat the oven to 375°F (190°C).

2. Place beaten eggs in a small dish. In another shallow dish, mix breadcrumbs with grated Parmesan cheese, chopped fresh basil, chopped fresh parsley, salt, and pepper.

3. Dip eggplant slices in beaten eggs, then coat them with the breadcrumb mixture, pressing lightly to adhere.

4. Heat olive oil in a large pan over medium-high heat. Fry eggplant slices in batches for 2-3 minutes on each side, or until golden brown. Add extra olive oil to the skillet as required.

5. Drain cooked eggplant slices on paper towels to remove excess oil.

6. Spread a thin layer of marinara sauce on the bottom of a baking dish. Arrange half of the fried eggplant slices on top of the sauce. Top with extra marinara sauce, then arrange the remaining eggplant pieces on top. Finish with a final coating of marinara sauce.

7. Top the eggplant with grated Parmesan cheese.

8. Bake in the preheated oven for 25–30 minutes, or until the sauce is bubbling and the cheese is melted and golden brown.

9. Remove it from the oven and allow it to cool slightly before serving.

QUICK TIPS

Serve Mediterranean eggplant parmesan with a side of whole wheat pasta or a mixed green salad. You may put a layer of mozzarella cheese on top before baking for an extra-cheesy variation.

7 MEDITERRANEAN STUFFED ZUCCHINI BOATS

Prep Time: 20 minutes Cooking Time: 30 minutes Total Time: 50 minutes Servings: 4

Ingredients

- 4 medium zucchinis
- 1 cup cooked quinoa;
- 1 can (15 ounces) chickpeas, drained and rinsed;
- 1 cup diced tomatoes;
- 1/2 cup diced red onion;
- 1/4 cup chopped fresh parsley;
- 1/4 cup crumbled feta cheese;
- 2 tablespoons extra-virgin olive oil;
- 2 tablespoons balsamic vinegar;
- 1 teaspoon dried oregano
- To taste, add salt and pepper.

Nutritional value:

- Calories: 220 kcal
- Fat: 8g
- Carbohydrates: 20g
- Fiber: 6g
- Protein: 15g

Directions

1. Preheat the oven to 375°F (190°C).
2. Slice each zucchini in half lengthwise. Use a spoon to scoop out the seeds and create a hollow core, producing "boats."
3. In a large mixing bowl, add cooked quinoa, chickpeas, diced tomatoes, red onion, parsley, and crumbled feta cheese.
4. In a separate bowl, mix together extra-virgin olive oil, balsamic vinegar, dried oregano, salt, and pepper to create the dressing.
5. Pour the dressing over the quinoa mixture and toss lightly to coat.
6. Spoon the quinoa mixture equally into each zucchini boat, pushing down gently to pack it in.
7. Place the packed zucchini boats, cut side up, on a baking dish.
8. Cover the baking dish with aluminum foil and bake for 20 minutes.
9. Remove the cover and bake for a further 10 minutes, or until the zucchini is soft and the filling is cooked through.
10. Serve hot, topped with additional chopped parsley if preferred.

QUICK TIPS

You may personalize the filling by adding items like chopped olives, artichoke hearts, or pine nuts. Leftover-ffilled zucchini boats may be kept in the refrigerator for up to 3 days and warmed in the oven or microwave before serving.

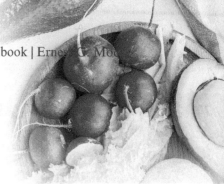

8 MEDITERRANEAN LENTIL SOUP

Prep Time: 15 minutes Cooking Time: 40 minutes Total Time: 55 minutes Servings: 6

Ingredients

- 1 tablespoon of olive oil 1 onion,
- chopped 2 carrots,
- diced 2 celery stalks,
- diced 3 cloves garlic, minced
- 1 cup dry green lentils
- 6 cups vegetarian broth;
- 1 can (14.5 ounces) chopped tomatoes;
- 2 teaspoons ground cumin;

- 1 teaspoon powdered turmeric;
- 1 teaspoon paprika
- Salt and pepper to taste;
- fresh lemon wedges for serving;
- chopped fresh parsley for garnish

Nutritional value:
- Calories: 220 kcal
- Fat: 5g
- Carbohydrates: 35g
- Fiber: 12g
- Protein: 12g

Directions

1. In a big saucepan, heat olive oil over medium heat. Add chopped onion, diced carrots, and diced celery. Cook for 5-7 minutes, or until veggies are softened.

2. Add minced garlic to the saucepan and simmer for an additional 1-2 minutes, stirring regularly.

3. Rinse dry green lentils under cold water and drain. Add them to the saucepan alongside vegetable broth, diced tomatoes (with their juices), ground cumin, ground turmeric, paprika, salt, and pepper. Stir to mix.

4. Bring the soup to a boil, then decrease the heat to medium and simmer for 30–35 minutes, or until the lentils are cooked.

5. Taste and adjust seasoning as required.

6. Serve hot, topped with fresh lemon wedges and chopped parsley.

QUICK TIPS

For a creamier texture, mix a part of the soup with an immersion blender before serving.
Serve Mediterranean Lentil Soup with crusty whole-grain bread or a side salad for a full meal.

9 MEDITERRANEAN STUFFED BELL PEPPERS WITH GROUND TURKEY

Prep Time: 20 minutes *Cooking Time: 45 minutes* *Total Time: 1 hour 5 minutes* *Servings: 4*

Ingredients

- 4 big bell peppers, halved and seeds removed;
- 1 tablespoon olive oil;
- 1 onion, diced;
- 2 cloves garlic, minced
- 1 pound lean ground turkey;
- 1 cup cooked quinoa;
- 1 can (15 ounces) chopped tomatoes, drained

- 1 teaspoon dried oregano
- 1 teaspoon dried basil; salt and pepper to taste;
- 1/2 cup shredded mozzarella cheese;
- And fresh basil leaves for garnish (optional).

Nutritional value:
- Calories: 320 kcal
- Fat: 12g
- Carbohydrates: 25g
- Fiber: 6g
- Protein: 25g

Directions

1. Preheat the oven to 375°F (190°C).
2. Heat olive oil in a large pan over medium heat. Add chopped onion and minced garlic, and sauté until softened, approximately 2–3 minutes.
3. Add ground turkey to the pan and heat until browned, breaking it up with a spoon as it cooks.
4. Stir in cooked quinoa, chopped tomatoes, dried oregano, dry basil, salt, and pepper. Cook for another 2-3 minutes to blend flavors.
5. Spoon the turkey-quinoa mixture equally into each bell pepper half, pushing down gently to compress it in.

6. Place the filled bell peppers on a baking tray, cut side up.
7. Cover the baking dish with aluminum foil and bake for 30 minutes.
8. Remove the foil and sprinkle shredded mozzarella cheese over the top of each filled pepper. Bake for an additional 15 minutes, or until the cheese is melted and bubbling.
9. Remove from the oven and allow the filled peppers to cool slightly before serving.
10. Garnish with fresh basil leaves if wanted, and serve hot.

QUICK TIPS

You may use any color of bell peppers for this dish or a variety of colors for a dynamic appearance. Leftover stuffed peppers may be kept in the refrigerator for up to 3 days and warmed in the oven or microwave before serving.

10 MEDITERRANEAN CHICKEN & VEGETABLE SKILLET

Prep Time: 15 minutes Cooking Time: 25 minutes Total Time: 40 minutes Servings: 4

Ingredients

- 1 tablespoon of olive oil 4 boneless,
- skinless chicken breasts,
- sliced into bite-sized pieces
- 1 onion, sliced
- 2 bell peppers (any color), sliced 1 zucchini, sliced 1 cup cherry tomatoes, halved
- 2 cloves garlic, minced
- 1 teaspoon dried oregano

- 1 teaspoon dried basil;
- salt and pepper to taste;
- juice of 1 lemon
- chopped fresh parsley for garnish

Nutritional value:
- Calories: 280 kcal
- Fat: 10g
- Carbohydrates: 15g
- Fiber: 4g
- Protein: 30g

Directions

1. Heat olive oil in a large pan over medium-high heat. Add chicken pieces and fry until browned on both sides, approximately 5–6 minutes. Remove the chicken from the pan and set it aside.

2. In the same pan, add the sliced onion and simmer until softened, approximately 3–4 minutes.

3. Add sliced bell peppers, sliced zucchini, half cherry tomatoes, minced garlic, dried oregano, dried basil, salt, and pepper to the pan. Cook for another 5–6 minutes, or until the veggies are soft.

4. Return the cooked chicken to the pan and toss to mix with the veggies.

5. Squeeze lemon juice over the chicken and vegetable mixture, and toss lightly to coat.

6. Cook for a further 2–3 minutes to heat thoroughly.

7. Garnish with chopped fresh parsley before serving.

8. Serve hot, either on its own or with a serving of whole-grain couscous or quinoa.

QUICK TIPS

Feel free to add additional veggies, such as mushrooms, eggplant, or asparagus, to the skillet according to your preference. - This recipe is adaptable and may be readily altered with your preferred herbs and spices.

CHAPTER 4
SNACK AND APPETIZER

1 MEDITERRANEAN HUMMUS PLATTER

Prep Time: 10 minutes Total Time: 10 minutes Servings: 4

Ingredients

- 1 cup hummus (store-bought or homemade)
- 1/2 cup cherry tomatoes, halved 1/2 cucumber, sliced
- 1/4 cup Kalamata olives
- 1/4 cup feta cheese, crumbled 1 tablespoon extra-virgin olive oil; 1 teaspoon dried oregano
- Whole-ggrain pita bread or crackers for serving

Nutritional value:
- Calories: 200 kcal
- Fat: 10g
- Carbohydrates: 20g
- Fiber: 6g
- Protein: 8g

Directions

1. Arrange hummus in the middle of a serving tray or shallow dish.

2. Surround the hummus with cherry tomatoes, cucumber slices, Kalamata olives, and crumbled feta cheese.

3. Drizzle extra-virgin olive oil over the hummus.

4. Sprinkle dry oregano over the whole plate.

5. Serve with whole-grain pita bread or crackers on the side.

6. Enjoy this tasty and healthful Mediterranean-inspired snack!

QUICK TIPS

Feel free to add additional veggies, such as mushrooms, eggplant, or asparagus, to the skillet according to your preference. - This recipe is adaptable and may be readily altered with your preferred herbs and spices.

2 MEDITERRANEAN STUFFED GRAPE LEAVES

Ingredients

- 1 jar (approximately 8 ounces) of grape leaves in brine, drained
- 1 cup cooked quinoa or rice
- 1/2 cup pine nuts, toasted
- 1/4 cup of currants or raisins
- 2 tablespoons extra-virgin olive oil;
- 2 teaspoons fresh lemon juice
- 2 cloves garlic, minced
- 1 teaspoon dried dill; 1 teaspoon dried mint
- To taste, add salt and pepper.
- Greek yogurt or tzatziki sauce for serving (optional)

Nutritional value:

- Calories: 120 kcal
- Fat: 6g
- Carbohydrates: 15g
- Fiber: 3g
- Protein: 2g

Directions

1. In a large mixing bowl, add cooked quinoa or rice, toasted pine nuts, currants or raisins, extra-virgin olive oil, fresh lemon juice, chopped garlic, dried dill, dried mint, salt, and pepper. Mix thoroughly to mix.

2. On a clean work surface, lay a grape leaf flat, smooth side down and rib side up. Place roughly 1 spoonful of the quinoa or rice mixture toward the leaf's stem end.

3. Fold the leaf's edges over the filling, then roll it up firmly from the stem end to the tip to create a compact cylinder. Repeat with the remaining grape leaves and filling.

4. Place packed grape leaves, seam side down, in a large pan or pot in a single layer, squeezing them firmly together.

5. Pour enough water over the filled grape leaves to slightly cover them.

6. To keep the grape leaves immersed in water, place a heatproof plate upside down on top of them.

7. Bring the water to a boil, then decrease the heat to low and simmer for 30 minutes, or until the grape leaves are soft.

8. Remove the dish and gently transfer the packed grape leaves to a serving tray using a slotted spoon.

9. Serve hot or at room temperature, with Greek yogurt or tzatziki sauce on the side, if desired.

QUICK TIPS

You may add chopped fresh herbs like parsley or mint to the filling for added taste.
Leftover filled grape leaves may be kept in the refrigerator for up to 3 days. They may be served cold or warmed slightly before serving.

3 MEDITERRANEAN GREEK SALAD SKEWERS

Prep Time: 15 minutes Total Time: 15 minutes Servings: Makes around 12 skewers

Ingredients

- 1 cup of cherry tomatoes
- 1 cucumber, sliced into bits
- 1/2 cup Kalamata olives
- 1/2 cup feta cheese, cubed 12 tiny, fresh basil leaves
- 2 tablespoons extra-virgin olive oil
- 1 tablespoon balsamic vinegar
- Salt and pepper to taste; toothpicks or tiny skewers

Nutritional value:
- Calories: 120 kcal
- Fat: 8g
- Carbohydrates: 10g
- Fiber: 2g
- Protein: 4g

Directions

1. Thread one cherry tomato, one cucumber chunk, one Kalamata olive, one cube of feta cheese, and one fresh basil leaf onto each toothpick or skewer, repeating until all ingredients are utilized.
2. Arrange the skewers on a serving plate.
3. In a separate bowl, mix together extra-virgin olive oil, balsamic vinegar, salt, and pepper to create the dressing.
4. Drizzle the dressing over the skewers, or offer it on the side for dipping.
5. Serve immediately and enjoy these bite-sized Greek salad skewers!

QUICK TIPS

You may modify these skewers by adding additional items such as marinated artichoke hearts, roasted red peppers, or grilled chicken. If using wooden skewers, soak them in water for at least 30 minutes before threading the ingredients to prevent them from scorching on the grill.

4 MEDITERRANEAN STUFFED MUSHROOMS

Prep Time: 20 minutes Cooking Time: 20 minutes Total Time: 40 minutes Servings: It makes approximately 12 stuffed mushrooms.

Ingredients

- 12 big button mushrooms, stems removed, and conserved
- 1 tablespoon of olive oil 2 cloves garlic, minced
- 1/4 cup minced red onion 1/2 cup chopped mushroom stems
- 1/2 cup chopped spinach; 1/4 cup grated Parmesan cheese; 1/4 cup breadcrumbs (use whole wheat breadcrumbs for a healthy choice).
- 2 teaspoons chopped fresh parsley
- To taste, add salt and pepper.

Nutritional value:
- Calories: 150 kcal
- Fat: 10g
- Carbohydrates: 8g
- Fiber: 2g
- Protein: 7g

Directions

1. Preheat the oven to 375°F (190°C). Line a baking sheet with parchment paper.
2. Place mushroom caps on the prepared baking sheet, hollow side up.
3. In a pan, heat olive oil over medium heat. Add minced garlic and chopped red onion, and sauté until softened, approximately 2–3 minutes.
4. In a skillet, add chopped mushroom stems and chopped spinach. Cook for another 3–4 minutes, or until the mushrooms release their liquid and the spinach wilts.

5. Remove the pan from heat and toss in grated Parmesan cheese, breadcrumbs, chopped fresh parsley, salt, and pepper.
6. Spoon the filling into the mushroom caps, pushing down slightly to compress it in.
7. Bake in the preheated oven for 15-20 minutes, or until the mushrooms are soft and the filling is golden brown.
8. Remove from the oven and allow the filled mushrooms to cool slightly before serving.
9. Serve hot and enjoy these delectable Mediterranean-filled mushrooms!

QUICK TIPS

You may add additional ingredients to the filling, such as diced tomatoes, chopped olives, or crumbled feta cheese, for more taste.
Leftover-filled mushrooms may be kept in an airtight jar in the refrigerator for up to 3 days. Prior to serving, reheat them in the oven or microwave.

5 MEDITERRANEAN ROASTED RED PEPPER HUMMUS

Prep Time: 10 minutes Cooking Time: 25 minutes (for roasting peppers) Total Time: 35 minutes
Servings: Makes around 2 cups

Ingredients

- 2 big red bell peppers
- 1 can (15 ounces) chickpeas, drained and rinsed 2 cloves garlic, minced
- 1/4 cup tahini, 2 tablespoons extra-virgin olive oil,
- and 2 teaspoons fresh lemon juice
- 1/2 teaspoon ground cumin; salt and pepper to taste;
- chopped fresh parsley and extra-virgin olive oil for garnish;
- whole grain pita bread or veggie sticks for serving

Nutritional value:

- Calories: 70 kcal
- Fat: 4g
- Carbohydrates: 7g
- Fiber: 2g
- Protein: 2g

Directions

1. Preheat the oven to 400°F (200°C). Line a baking sheet with parchment paper.

2. Place the entire red bell peppers on the prepared baking sheet and roast in the preheated oven for 20–25 minutes, or until the peppers are roasted and softened, turning them periodically.

3. Remove the roasted peppers from the oven and allow them to cool slightly. Once cool enough to handle, peel off the charred skin, remove the seeds, and cut the meat.

4. In a food processor, add roasted red peppers, drained and rinsed chickpeas, chopped garlic, tahini, extra-virgin olive oil, fresh lemon juice, ground cumin, salt, and pepper.

5. Blend until smooth and creamy, scraping down the sides of the food processor as required.

6. Taste and adjust seasoning as required.

7. Transfer the roasted red pepper hummus to a serving dish. Drizzle with extra-virgin olive oil and sprinkle with chopped fresh parsley.

8. Serve with whole-grain pita bread or veggie sticks for dipping.

QUICK TIPS

You may modify the taste by adding ingredients like roasted garlic, smoky paprika, or chopped fresh herbs like cilantro or basil. Store leftover roasted red pepper hummus in an airtight jar in the refrigerator for up to 5 days. Stir thoroughly before serving.

6 MEDITERRANEAN BRUSCHETTA WITH TOMATO AND BASIL

Prep Time: 15 minutes Cooking Time: 5 minutes Total Time: 20 minutes Servings: It makes approximately 12 pieces.

Ingredients

- 1 French baguette, cut into 1/2-inch-thick pieces 2 big,
- ripe tomatoes,
- diced 2 cloves garlic, minced
- 1/4 cup chopped fresh basil;
- 2 tablespoons extra-virgin olive oil;
- 1 tablespoon balsamic vinegar;
- salt and pepper to taste; grated Parmesan cheese for garnish (optional)

Nutritional value:

- Calories: 120 kcal
- Fat: 5g
- Carbohydrates: 15g
- Fiber: 2g
- Protein: 3g

Directions

1. Preheat the oven broiler on high.
2. Place baguette slices on a baking pan and toast them in the broiler for 2-3 minutes on each side, or until softly golden brown.
3. In a mixing bowl, add diced tomatoes, minced garlic, chopped fresh basil, extra-virgin olive oil, balsamic vinegar, salt, and pepper. Mix thoroughly to mix.

4. Spoon the tomato mixture equally over the toasted baguette pieces.
5. If desired, sprinkle grated Parmesan cheese on top of each bruschetta.
6. Serve immediately as a wonderful Mediterranean snack.

QUICK TIPS

Tips: For extra taste, you may sprinkle the toasted baguette slices with a clove of garlic before topping them with the tomato mixture. Experiment with various types of tomatoes, such as heirloom or cherry tomatoes, for a fresh take on standard bruschetta.

CHAPTER 5
POULTRY DISHES

1 MEDITERRANEAN LEMON HERB GRILLED CHICKEN

Prep Time: 10 minutes Marinating Time: 2 hours Cooking Time: 15 minutes Total Time: 2 hours 25 minutes
Servings: 4

Ingredients

- 4 boneless, skinless chicken breasts
- zest and juice of 1 lemon
- 2 cloves garlic, minced
- 2 tablespoons extra-virgin olive oil;
- 1 teaspoon dried oregano;
- 1 teaspoon dried thyme;
- salt and pepper to taste;
- Lemon wedges for serving;
- And chopped fresh parsley for garnish.

Nutritional value:
- Calories: 250 kcal
- Fat: 12g
- Carbohydrates: 2g
- Fiber: 0g
- Protein: 30g

Directions

1. In a small bowl, mix together lemon zest, lemon juice, minced garlic, extra-virgin olive oil, dried oregano, dried thyme, salt, and pepper to form the marinade.

2. Place chicken breasts in a shallow dish or resealable plastic bag. Pour the marinade over the chicken, ensuring it is uniformly covered. Cover or seal and refrigerate for at least 2 hours, preferably overnight, for optimal effects.

3. Preheat the grill to medium-high heat. Remove the chicken from the marinade and discard any extra marinade.

4. Grill chicken breasts for 6-7 minutes on each side, or until cooked through and no longer pink in the middle, with an internal temperature of 165°F (75°C).

5. Remove from the grill and allow the chicken to rest for a few minutes before slicing.

6. Serve hot, topped with chopped fresh parsley and lemon wedges on the side.

Tips: For extra taste, you may add a sprinkle of crushed red pepper flakes to the marinade for a bit of fire.
Make sure to let the chicken marinade for at least 2 hours to enable the aromas to infiltrate the flesh.

54

2 MEDITERRANEAN BAKED CHICKEN WITH OLIVES AND TOMATOES

Prep Time: 15 minutes Cooking Time: 35 minutes Total Time: 50 minutes Servings: 4

Ingredients

- 4 bone-in, skin-on chicken thighs
- Salt and pepper to taste;
- 2 tablespoons extra-virgin olive oil 1 onion, thinly sliced;
- 2 cloves garlic, minced
- 1 can (14.5 ounces) of chopped tomatoes, drained
- 1/2 cup Kalamata olives, pitted 1 teaspoon dried oregano
- 1 teaspoon dried thyme;
- 1/4 cup chopped fresh parsley for garnish

Nutritional value:
- Calories: 280 kcal
- Fat: 15g
- Carbohydrates: 6g
- Fiber: 2g
- Protein: 30g

Directions

1. Preheat the oven to 375°F (190°C).

2. Season chicken thighs with salt and pepper on both sides.

3. Heat extra-virgin olive oil in an oven-safe skillet over medium-high heat. Add chicken thighs, skin side down, and cook for 5–6 minutes, or until golden brown. Flip and cook for a further 3–4 minutes on the other side. Remove the chicken from the pan and set it aside.

4. In the same pan, add thinly sliced onion and chopped garlic. Cook for 2-3 minutes, or until softened.

5. Stir in diced tomatoes, Kalamata olives, dry oregano, and dried thyme. Cook for another 2-3 minutes, stirring periodically.

6. Return the chicken thighs to the pan, skin side up, nestling them into the tomato mixture.

7. Transfer the pan to the preheated oven and bake for 25–30 minutes, or until the chicken is cooked through and the juices run clear.

8. Remove from the oven and allow the chicken to rest for a few minutes before serving.

9. Sprinkle chopped fresh parsley over the chicken before serving.

QUICK TIPS

You may use chicken breasts instead of chicken thighs if desired. Adjust the cooking time appropriately, as chicken breasts may cook quicker. Serve this fragrant Mediterranean roasted chicken with a side of couscous or quinoa and steamed veggies for a full supper.

3 MEDITERRANEAN TURKEY MEATBALLS IN TOMATO SAUCE

Prep Time: 15 minutes Cooking Time: 25 minutes Total Time: 40 minutes Servings: It makes approximately 20 meatballs.

Ingredients

FOR THE MEATBALLS:

- 1 pound ground turkey; 1/2 cup breadcrumbs (use whole wheat breadcrumbs for a healthier choice)
- 1/4 cup grated Parmesan cheese
- 1/4 cup chopped fresh parsley
- 1 egg, beaten
- 2 cloves garlic, minced
- 1 teaspoon dried oregano
- 1 teaspoon dried basil
- To taste, add salt and pepper.

FOR THE TOMATO SAUCE:

1 can (14.5 ounces) of chopped tomatoes 1 onion, diced 2 cloves garlic, minced
2 tablespoons extra-virgin olive oil; 1 teaspoon dried oregano
1 teaspoon dried basil
To taste, add salt and pepper.

> **Nutritional value:**
> - Calories: 280 kcal
> - Fat: 12g
> - Carbohydrates: 15g
> - Fiber: 3g
> - Protein: 25g

Directions

1. Preheat the oven to 400°F (200°C). Line a baking sheet with parchment paper.

2. In a large mixing bowl, add ground turkey, breadcrumbs, grated Parmesan cheese, chopped fresh parsley, beaten egg, minced garlic, dried oregano, dried basil, salt, and pepper. Mix thoroughly to mix.

3. Shape the turkey mixture into meatballs, approximately 1 inch in diameter, and set them on the prepared baking sheet.

4. Bake in the preheated oven for 20–25 minutes, or until the meatballs are cooked through and browned on the exterior.

5. While the meatballs are baking, make the tomato sauce. In a pan, heat extra-virgin olive oil over medium heat. Add chopped onion and minced garlic, and heat until softened, approximately 3–4 minutes.

6. Stir in chopped tomatoes (with their juices), dried oregano, dry basil, salt, and pepper. Simmer for 10–15 minutes, stirring periodically, until the sauce thickens slightly.

7. Once the meatballs are cooked, put them in the pan with the tomato sauce. Gently toss to coat the meatballs with sauce.

8. Serve hot, garnished with more chopped parsley if preferred. Enjoy these tasty Mediterranean turkey meatballs!

QUICK TIPS

Serve the meatballs over cooked whole wheat spaghetti or zucchini noodles for a tasty and healthy meal. These meatballs may also be served as an appetizer with toothpicks for dipping into the tomato sauce.

4 MEDITERRANEAN CHICKEN SOUVLAKI WITH TZATZIKI SAUCE

Prep Time: 20 minutes Marinating Time: 1-2 hours Cooking Time: 10 minutes Total Time: 1 hour 30 minutes Servings: 4

Ingredients

FOR THE CHICKEN SKEWERS:

- 1 pound of boneless, skinless chicken breasts, cut into 1-inch cubes
- 1/4 cup extra-virgin olive oil
- 2 teaspoons of fresh lemon juice
- 2 cloves garlic, minced
- 1 teaspoon dried oregano
- 1 teaspoon dried thyme; salt and pepper to taste; wooden or metal skewers

FOR THE TZATZIKI SAUCE:

- 1 cup Greek yogurt
- 1/2 cucumber, grated and pressed to remove extra moisture
- 1 clove garlic, minced
- 1 tablespoon of fresh lemon juice
- 1 tablespoon chopped fresh dill (or 1 teaspoon dried dill)
- To taste, add salt and pepper.

Nutritional value:

- Calories: 320 kcal
- Fat: 12g
- Carbohydrates: 15g
- Fiber: 2g
- Protein: 30g

Directions

1. In a mixing bowl, add extra-virgin olive oil, fresh lemon juice, minced garlic, dried oregano, dried thyme, salt, and pepper to prepare the marinade.
2. Add chicken cubes to the marinade and toss to coat. Cover and refrigerate for 1-2 hours to marinate.
3. If using wooden skewers, soak them in water for at least 30 minutes to avoid scorching.
4. Preheat the grill to medium-high heat.
5. Thread marinated chicken chunks onto skewers, dividing equally.
6. Grill chicken skewers for 4-5 minutes on each side, or until cooked through and golden brown with grill marks.

7. While the chicken is cooking, make the tzatziki sauce. In a small bowl, add Greek yogurt, grated cucumber, minced garlic, fresh lemon juice, chopped fresh dill, salt, and pepper. Mix thoroughly to mix.
8. Serve the grilled chicken skewers hot, followed with tzatziki sauce for dipping.

QUICK TIPS

Serve the chicken souvlaki with a side of warm pita bread, Greek salad, and roasted veggies for a full Mediterranean meal. You may also add sliced bell peppers, red onions, or cherry tomatoes to the skewers for more taste and color.

5 MEDITERRANEAN LEMON HERB ROAST CHICKEN

Prep Time: 15 minutes Cooking Time: 1 hour 30 minutes Total Time: 1 hour 45 minutes Servings: 4-6

Ingredients

- 1 entire chicken (approximately) (4-5 pounds)
- 1 lemon, halved
- 4 cloves garlic, minced
- 2 tablespoons extra-virgin olive oil;
- 2 teaspoons chopped fresh parsley;
- 1 tablespoon chopped fresh rosemary;
- 1 tablespoon chopped fresh thyme
- Salt and pepper to taste 1 onion, quartered;
- 1 carrot, chopped;
- 1 celery stalk, chopped;
- 1 cup chicken broth

Nutritional value:

- Calories: 350 kcal
- Fat: 18g
- Carbohydrates: 4g
- Fiber: 1g
- Protein: 40g

Directions

1. Preheat the oven to 375°F (190°C). Rinse the chicken inside and out under cold running water, and wipe dry with paper towels.

2. Squeeze the juice of one lemon over the chicken, then insert the lemon halves within the cavity.

3. In a small bowl, add minced garlic, extra-virgin olive oil, chopped fresh parsley, chopped fresh rosemary, chopped fresh thyme, salt, and pepper to produce the herb combination.

4. Rub the herb mixture all over the surface of the chicken, ensuring it is uniformly covered.

5. Place the quartered onion, diced carrot, and chopped celery in the bottom of a roasting pan or big baking dish. Place the seasoned chicken on top.

6. Pour chicken stock into the bottom of the roasting pan.

7. Roast the chicken in the preheated oven for 1 hour and 30 minutes to 1 hour and 45 minutes, or until the juices flow clear when the thickest portion of the thigh is punctured with a skewer and the internal temperature reaches 165°F (75°C).

8. If the chicken begins to brown too rapidly, tent it gently with aluminum foil.

9. Once done, take the chicken from the oven and let it rest for 10–15 minutes before cutting.

10. Carve the chicken and serve hot, surrounded by roasted veggies and your favorite side dishes.

QUICK TIPS

For added flavor, you may add slices of lemon, garlic cloves, and fresh herbs inside the cavity of the chicken before roasting. Use any leftover chicken bones to create homemade chicken broth for soups or stews. Simply boil the bones with water, veggies, and herbs for a few hours, then filter the liquid to remove solids.

CHAPTER

6

DESSERT

1 MEDITERRANEAN ORANGE AND ALMOND CAKE

Prep Time: 15 minutes Cooking Time: 45 minutes Total Time: 1 hour Servings: 8

Ingredients

- 2 big oranges and 4 eggs
- 1 cup of almond meal
- 1/2 cup honey
- 1 teaspoon baking powder
- 1/2 teaspoon vanilla extract
- Powdered sugar for dusting (optional)

Nutritional value:
- Calories: 250 kcal
- Fat: 15g
- Carbohydrates: 25g
- Fiber: 3g
- Protein: 6g

Directions

1. Preheat the oven to 350°F (175°C). Grease a 9-inch round cake pan and cover the bottom with parchment paper.

2. Wash the oranges carefully and throw them in a saucepan. Cover with water and bring to a boil. Reduce the heat and simmer for 1 hour, or until the oranges are very soft.

3. Drain the oranges and let them cool somewhat. Cut them into quarters and remove any seeds.

4. Place the cooked oranges (with peel) in a food processor and pulse until smooth.

5. In a large mixing basin, whisk the eggs until pale and fluffy.

6. Add the pureed oranges, almond meal, honey, baking powder, and vanilla essence to the beaten eggs. Mix until completely blended.

7. Pour the batter into the prepared cake pan and level the top with a spatula.

8. Bake in the preheated oven for 40–45 minutes, or until the cake is golden brown and a toothpick inserted into the middle comes out clean.

9. Remove the cake from the oven and allow it to rest in the pan for 10 minutes before transferring it to a wire rack to cool fully.

10. Once cooled, sprinkle the top of the cake with powdered sugar if desired.

11. Slice and serve this rich and tasty Mediterranean orange and almond cake.

You may top the cake with sliced almonds or fresh berries for an added touch of elegance.
Leftover cake may be kept in an airtight jar at room temperature for up to 3 days.

2 MEDITERRANEAN YOGURT PARFAIT WITH HONEY AND PISTACHIOS

Prep Time: 10 minutes Total Time: 10 minutes Servings: 2

Ingredients

- 1 cup Greek yogurt
- 2 teaspoons of honey 1/4 cup chopped pistachios
- 1/2 cup mixed fresh berries (such as strawberries, blueberries, or raspberries)
- 1 tablespoon shredded coconut (optional)

Nutritional value:
- Calories: 200 kcal
- Fat: 8g
- Carbohydrates: 25g
- Fiber: 2g
- Protein: 10g

Directions

1. In two serving glasses or bowls, layer Greek yogurt, honey, chopped pistachios, and mixed fresh berries.

2. Repeat the layers until the glasses are full, culminating with a sprinkling of chopped pistachios on top.

3. If preferred, sprinkle with shredded coconut for extra taste and texture.

4. Serve immediately and enjoy this delicious and healthy Mediterranean yogurt parfait.

Feel free to personalize the parfait with your favorite nuts, seeds, and fruits. Sliced bananas, chopped mangoes, or pomegranate arils all make great additions. For a vegan variation, you may use dairy-free yogurt such as almond or coconut yogurt and replace maple syrup for honey.

3 MEDITERRANEAN LEMON OLIVE OIL CAKE

Prep Time: 15 minutes Cooking Time: 40 minutes Total Time: 55 minutes Servings: 8

Ingredients

- 1 1/2 cups all-purpose flour 1 teaspoon baking powder
- 1/2 teaspoon baking soda
- 1/4 teaspoon salt
- Zest of 2 lemons
- 1/2 cup fresh lemon juice
- 3/4 cup granulated sugar 1/2 cup extra-virgin olive oil
- 2 big eggs
- 1 teaspoon vanilla extract; powdered sugar for dusting (optional)

Nutritional value:
- Calories: 280 kcal
- Fat: 15g
- Carbohydrates: 35g
- Fiber: 1g
- Protein: 4g

Directions

1. Preheat the oven to 350°F (175°C). Grease a 9-inch round cake pan and cover the bottom with parchment paper.

2. In a larger basin, mix together the flour, baking powder, baking soda, and salt.

3. In a large bowl, mix together the lemon zest, lemon juice, granulated sugar, olive oil, eggs, and vanilla essence until thoroughly incorporated.

4. Gradually add the dry ingredients to the wet components, mixing until just mixed and no lumps remain.

5. Pour the batter into the prepared cake pan and level the top with a spatula.

6. Bake in the preheated oven for 35–40 minutes, or until a toothpick inserted into the middle of the cake comes out clean.

7. Remove the cake from the oven and allow it to rest in the pan for 10 minutes before transferring it to a wire rack to cool fully.

8. Once cooled, sprinkle the top of the cake with powdered sugar if desired.

9. Slice and serve this soft and fragrant Mediterranean lemon olive oil cake.

QUICK TIPS

For extra texture and taste, you may mix in 1/2 cup of coarsely chopped almonds or pistachios into the dough before baking. Leftover cake may be kept in an airtight jar at room temperature for up to 3 days.

4 MEDITERRANEAN HONEY NUT BAKLAVA

Prep Time: 30 minutes Cooking Time: 30 minutes Total Time: 1 hour Servings: It makes approximately 24 pieces.

Ingredients

- 1 package (16 ounces) of phyllo dough, thawed
- 1 cup unsalted butter, melted
- 2 cups mixed nuts (such as walnuts, pistachios, and almonds), finely chopped
- 1/2 cup granulated sugar; 1 teaspoon ground cinnamon
- 1/2 cup honey 1/4 cup water; 1 tablespoon fresh lemon juice

Nutritional value:

- Calories: 150 kcal
- Fat: 10g
- Carbohydrates: 15g
- Fiber: 1g
- Protein: 2g

Directions

1. Preheat the oven to 350°F (175°C). Grease a 9x13-inch baking dish.

2. In a medium bowl, mix the chopped nuts, granulated sugar, and ground cinnamon. Mix thoroughly and set aside.

3. Unroll the phyllo dough and cover it with a moist dish towel to keep it from drying out.

4. Place one sheet of phyllo dough in the prepared baking dish and brush it with melted butter. Repeat with 7 additional sheets of phyllo dough, brushing each sheet with butter.

5. Sprinkle approximately 1/3 cup of the nut mixture evenly over the phyllo dough.

6. Continue stacking the phyllo dough and nut mixture, coating each phyllo sheet with butter until all of the nut mixture is used.

7. Finish with a final layer of phyllo dough, coating the top sheet liberally with butter.

8. Using a sharp knife, gently cut the baklava into diamond or square shapes.

9. Bake in the preheated oven for 25–30 minutes, or until the baklava is golden brown and crispy.

10. While the baklava is baking, make the honey syrup. In a small saucepan, mix honey, water, and lemon juice. Bring to a boil, then decrease the heat and simmer for 5 minutes.

11. Remove the baklava from the oven and immediately pour the hot honey syrup evenly over the top.

12. Let the baklava cool fully in the pan before serving.

QUICK TIPS

Be careful to cover the phyllo dough with a moist cloth while working with it to avoid it from drying out and becoming brittle. For optimal results, leave the baklava to rest at room temperature for a few hours or overnight before serving to enable the flavors to combine and the syrup to soak into the layers.

5 MEDITERRANEAN FRUIT SALAD WITH HONEY-LIME DRESSING

Prep Time: 15 minutes Total Time: 15 minutes Servings: 4

Ingredients

- 2 cups mixed fresh fruit (such as strawberries, blueberries, grapes, kiwi, pineapple, and oranges), diced or sliced
- 1 tablespoon of honey
- One lime's juice
- 1 teaspoon lime zest; fresh mint leaves for garnish (optional)

Nutritional value:
- Calories: 120 kcal
- Fat: 0g
- Carbohydrates: 30g
- Fiber: 4g
- Protein: 2g

Directions

1. In a large mixing basin, add the assorted fresh fruit.

2. In a separate bowl, mix together the honey, lime juice, and lime zest to create the dressing.

3. Pour the dressing over the mixed fruit and toss lightly to coat.

4. Garnish with fresh mint leaves if preferred.

5. Serve immediately, or refrigerate until ready to serve.

QUICK TIPS

Feel free to use any mix of your favorite fresh fruits in this salad. Berries, citrus fruits, and tropical fruits work nicely together. You may also add a sprinkling of roasted nuts or coconut flakes for added crunch and flavor. This fruit salad is best served fresh, but it may be kept in an airtight container in the refrigerator for up to 2 days.

CHAPTER 7

STEW & SOUP

1 MEDITERRANEAN LENTIL SOUP

Prep Time: 10 minutes Cooking Time: 30 minutes Total Time: 40 minutes Servings: 6

Ingredients

- 1 tablespoon olive oil; 1 onion, chopped
- 2 carrots, diced 2 celery stalks, diced
- 3 cloves garlic, minced
- 1 cup dry green or brown lentils, washed
- 1 can (14.5 ounces) of chopped tomatoes
- 6 cups veggie broth or water
- 1 teaspoon dried oregano;
- 1 teaspoon dried thyme;
- salt and pepper to taste;
- fresh parsley for garnish

Nutritional value:
- Calories: 220 kcal
- Fat: 2g
- Carbohydrates: 38g
- Fiber: 10g
- Protein: 14g

Directions

1. Heat olive oil in a big saucepan over medium heat. Add chopped onion, carrots, and celery. Cook, stirring occasionally, for 5-7 minutes until veggies are softened.

2. Add minced garlic and heat for an additional minute until fragrant.

3. Stir in dry lentils, chopped tomatoes (with their juices), vegetable broth or water, dried oregano, dried thyme, salt, and pepper.

4. Bring the soup to a boil, then decrease the heat to low and allow it to simmer for 25–30 minutes, or until the lentils are cooked.

5. Taste and adjust seasoning as required.

6. Ladle the soup into dishes and sprinkle with fresh parsley before serving.

QUICK TIPS

You may add more veggies, like spinach, kale, or chopped potatoes, for added nutrition and taste. Serve the lentil soup with a piece of crusty bread or a side salad for a full and fulfilling dinner.

2 MEDITERRANEAN CHICKPEA STEW

Prep Time: 15 minutes Cooking Time: 45 minutes Total Time: 1 hour Servings: 4

Ingredients

- 2 tablespoons of olive oil 1 onion, diced 2 cloves garlic, minced
- 2 carrots, diced
- 2 celery stalks, chopped
- 1 red bell pepper, chopped
- 1 teaspoon ground cumin; 1 teaspoon smoked paprika
- 1/2 teaspoon ground coriander
- 1 can (14.5 ounces) of chopped tomatoes 2 cans (15 ounces each) of chickpeas, drained and rinsed
- 4 cups vegetable broth; salt and pepper to taste; and fresh parsley for garnish.

Nutritional value:
- Calories: 280 kcal
- Fat: 8g
- Carbohydrates: 40g
- Fiber: 10g
- Protein: 12g

Directions

. Heat olive oil in a big saucepan over medium heat. Add chopped onion and sauté until translucent, approximately 5 minutes.

2. Add minced garlic, chopped carrots, diced celery, and diced red bell pepper. Cook, stirring regularly, for another 5 minutes until the veggies are softened.

3. Stir in ground cumin, smoked paprika, and ground coriander. Cook for 1-2 minutes until aromatic.

4. In a saucepan, add chopped tomatoes (with their juices), drained and rinsed chickpeas, and vegetable broth. Season with salt and pepper, to taste.

5. Bring the stew to a boil, then decrease the heat to low and let it simmer uncovered for 30–40 minutes, stirring regularly, until the flavors have merged and the stew has thickened.

6. Taste and adjust seasoning as required.

7. Ladle the chickpea stew into dishes and sprinkle with fresh parsley before serving.

QUICK TIPS

You may add chopped spinach or kale to the stew during the final 5 minutes of simmering for extra greens. Serve the chickpea stew with cooked quinoa, brown rice, or crusty bread for a robust and fulfilling supper.

67

3 MEDITERRANEAN VEGETABLE STEW

Prep Time: 15 minutes Cooking Time: 40 minutes Total Time: 55 minutes Servings: 6

Ingredients

- 2tablespoons of tablespoons of olive oil 1 onion, diced 2 cloves garlic, minced 2 carrots,
- diced 2 celery stalks, diced 1 red bell pepper, diced;;
- 1 yellow bell pepper, diced;; 1 zucchini, diced;
- 1 yellow squash, diced;
- 1 can (14.5ounces) of ounces) of diced tomatoes
- 4 cups vegetable broth;
- 1 teaspoon dried oregano
- 1 teaspoon dried basil;
- Salt and pepper to taste; and fresh f parsley for garnish.

Nutritional value:
- Calories: 150 kcal
- Fat: 5g
- Carbohydrates: 25g
- Fiber: 7g
- Protein: 5g

Directions

1. Heat olive oil in a big saucepan over medium heat. Add chopped onion and sauté until translucent, approximately 5 minutes.

2. Add minced garlic, chopped carrots, diced celery, diced red bell pepper, and diced yellow bell pepper. Cook, stirring regularly, for another 5 minutes untilthe veggies the veggies are softened.

3. Stir in chopped zucchini and diced yellow squash. Cook for a further 3–53–5 minutes.

4. Add chopped tomatoes (with their juices), vegetable broth, dried oregano, dry basil, salt, and pepper to the saucepan.

5. Bring the stew to a boil, then decrease the heat to low and let it simmer uncovered for 25–3025–30 minutes, stirring regularly, until the veggies are cooked.

6. Taste and adjust seasoning as required.

7. Ladle the vegetable stew into dishes and sprinkle with fresh parsley before serving.

QUICK TIPS

Feel free to add different veggies, such as eggplant, green beans, or potatoes, according to your choice. Serve the vegetable stew with a piece of crusty bread or cooked grains such as quinoa or couscous for a full and healthy dinner.

4 MEDITERRANEAN FISH STEW

Ingredients

- 1 tablespoon olive oil; 1 onion, chopped
- 2 cloves garlic, minced
- 1 fennel bulb, finely sliced 1 red bell pepper, diced
- 1 yellow bell pepper, chopped
- 1 can (14.5 ounces) of chopped tomatoes
- 4 cups fish or seafood broth;
- 1 teaspoon dried thyme;
- 1 teaspoon dried oregano 1 bay leaf;
- 1pound of white fish fillets (such as cod or halibut), cut into bits
- Salt and pepper to taste; fresh parsley for garnish

Nutritional value:
- Calories: 220 kcal
- Fat: 8g
- Carbohydrates: 10g
- Fiber: 3g
- Protein: 25g

Directions

1. Heat olive oil in a big saucepan over medium heat. Add chopped onion and sauté until translucent, approximately 5 minutes.

2. Add minced garlic, thinly sliced fennel bulb, chopped red bell pepper, and diced yellow bell pepper. Cook, stirring regularly, for another 5 minutes until the veggies are softened.

3. Stir in chopped tomatoes (with their juices), fish or seafood broth, dried thyme, dry oregano, and bay leaf. Bring the stew to a boil.

4. Reduce the heat to low and let the stew simmer uncovered for 15-20 minutes to enable the flavors to blend.

5. Add the pieces of white fish to the saucepan and boil for an additional 5–7 minutes, or until the fish is cooked through and opaque.

6. Season the fish stew with salt and pepper, to taste.

7. Ladle the fish stew into dishes and sprinkle with fresh parsley before serving.

QUICK TIPS

You may add different seafood, such as shrimp, mussels, or scallops, to the stew for more flavor and diversity. Serve the fish stew with crusty bread or cooked grains such as rice or quinoa for a full and healthy supper.

5 MEDITERRANEAN BEAN SOUP

Prep Time: 15 minutes Cooking Time: 1 hour Total Time: 1 hour 15 minutes Servings: 6

Ingredients

- 2 tablespoons of olive oil 1 onion, diced 2 carrots, diced 2 celery stalks, chopped
- 3 cloves garlic, minced
- 1 teaspoon dried thyme; 1 teaspoon dry oregano
- 1 bay leaf; 1 can (14.5 ounces) of chopped tomatoes
- 6 cups vegetable broth; 2 cans (15 ounces each) cannellini beans, washed and rinsed
- Salt and pepper to taste; fresh parsley for garnish

Nutritional value:
- Calories: 180 kcal
- Fat: 2g
- Carbohydrates: 30g
- Fiber: 8g
- Protein: 10g

Directions

1. Heat olive oil in a big saucepan over medium heat. Add chopped onion, carrots, and celery. Cook, stirring occasionally, for 5-7 minutes until veggies are softened.

2. Add minced garlic, dried thyme, dry oregano, and bay leaf. Cook for another 1-2 minutes until aromatic.

3. Stir in chopped tomatoes (with their juices) and veggie broth. Bring the soup to a boil.

4. Reduce the heat to low and let the soup simmer uncovered for 30–40 minutes, stirring regularly.

5. Add drained and washed cannellini beans to the saucepan and simmer for a further 10–15 minutes until cooked through.

6. To taste, season the bean soup with salt and pepper.

7. Ladle the bean soup into dishes and sprinkle with fresh parsley before serving.

QUICK TIPS

You may use any sort of bean, such as navy beans, kidney beans, or chickpeas, in this soup according to your choice. Serve the bean soup with a drizzle of extra-virgin olive oil and a sprinkling of grated Parmesan cheese for enhanced taste.

CHAPTER 8

VEGETARIAN

1 MEDITERRANEAN STUFFED BELL PEPPERS

Prep Time: 20 minutes Cooking Time: 40 minutes Total Time: 1 hour Servings: 4

Ingredients

- 4 big bell peppers (any color), halved and seeds removed 1 cup quinoa, washed
- 2 cups veggie broth, 1 tablespoon olive oil
- 1 onion, diced
- 2 cloves garlic, minced
- 1 zucchini, diced 1 yellow squash, diced
- 1 cup cherry tomatoes, halved
- 1 cup canned chickpeas, drained and rinsed
- 1 teaspoon dried oregano
- 1 teaspoon dried basil; salt and pepper to taste; 1/2 cup crumbled feta cheese (optional)
- Fresh parsley for garnish

Nutritional value:
- Calories: 250 kcal
- Fat: 8g
- Carbohydrates: 35g
- Fiber: 8g
- Protein: 12g

Directions

1. Preheat the oven to 375°F (190°C). Arrange the half-bell peppers on a baking dish, cut side up.
2. In a medium saucepan, mix the quinoa and vegetable broth. Bring to a boil, then decrease heat to low, cover, and simmer for 15-20 minutes, or until quinoa is cooked and liquid is absorbed.
3. In a large pan, heat olive oil over medium heat. Add chopped onion and sauté until translucent, approximately 5 minutes.
4. Add minced garlic, diced zucchini, and diced yellow squash to the skillet. Cook, stirring regularly, for another 5 minutes until the veggies are softened.
5. Stir in halved cherry tomatoes, drained and rinsed chickpeas, dried oregano, dried basil, cooked quinoa, salt, and pepper. Cook for a further 2–3 minutes to blend flavors.
6. Spoon the quinoa and vegetable mixture equally into the split bell peppers, pushing slightly to compact the contents.
7. Cover the baking dish with aluminum foil and bake in the preheated oven for 25–30 minutes, or until the peppers are soft.
8. If using, sprinkle crumbled feta cheese over the filled peppers during the final 5 minutes of baking.
9. Remove the filled peppers from the oven and allow them to cool slightly before serving.
10. Garnish with fresh parsley before serving.

QUICK TIPS

Feel free to modify the filling using your favorite veggies and seasonings.
Leftover stuffed peppers may be kept in an airtight jar in the refrigerator for up to 3 days

2 MEDITERRANEAN EGGPLANT PARMESAN

Prep Time: 30 minutes Cooking Time: 45 minutes Total Time: 1 hour 15 minutes Servings: 4

Ingredients

- 2 medium eggplants, cut into 1/4-inch circles
- Salt
- 2 cups marinara sauce
- 1 cup breadcrumbs (use whole wheat breadcrumbs for a healthier choice)
- 1/2 cup grated Parmesan cheese
- 2 eggs, beaten
- 1 cup shredded mozzarella cheese
- Fresh basil leaves for garnish

Nutritional value:
- Calories: 320 kcal
- Fat: 18g
- Carbohydrates: 30g
- Fiber: 8g
- Protein: 12g

Directions

1. Place the eggplant slices in a colander and sprinkle them with salt. Let them sit for 20–30 minutes to remove extra moisture. Pat the eggplant slices dry with paper towels.

2. Preheat the oven to 375°F (190°C). Grease a baking sheet with olive oil.

3. Set up a breading station: in one shallow dish, lay beaten eggs; in another shallow dish, mix breadcrumbs and grated Parmesan cheese.

4. Dip each eggplant slice into the beaten eggs, then coat equally with the breadcrumb mixture. Place the breaded eggplant slices on the prepared baking sheet.

5. Bake the breaded eggplant slices in the preheated oven for 20–25 minutes, or until golden brown and crispy.

6. Remove the roasted eggplant slices from the oven and decrease the oven temperature to 350°F (175°C).

7. Spread a thin layer of marinara sauce on the bottom of a baking dish. Arrange half of the cooked eggplant slices in a single layer over the marinara sauce.

8. Spoon extra marinara sauce over the eggplant pieces, then top with shredded mozzarella cheese. Repeat with the remaining eggplant pieces, marinara sauce, and mozzarella cheese.

9. Cover the baking dish with aluminum foil and bake in the preheated oven for 20–25 minutes, or until the cheese is melted and bubbling.

10. Remove the aluminum foil and bake for a further 5 minutes to gently brown the cheese.

11. Remove the eggplant Parmesan from the oven and allow it to cool slightly before serving

12. Garnish with fresh basil leaves before serving.

QUICK TIPS

Serve the eggplant Parmesan with cooked spaghetti or a side salad for a full dinner.
You may create the marinara sauce from scratch or use store-bought marinara sauce for convenience.

3 MEDITERRANEAN SPINACH & FETA STUFFED PORTOBELLO MUSHROOMS

Prep Time: 20 minutes Cooking Time: 25 minutes Total Time: 45 minutes Servings: 4

Ingredients

- 4 big portobello mushrooms, stems removed;
- 2 tablespoons olive oil;
- 1 onion, finely chopped; 2 cloves garlic, minced
- 4 cups of fresh spinach leaves
- 1/2 cup crumbled feta cheese
- 1/4 cup grated Parmesan cheese
- Salt and pepper to taste; fresh parsley for garnish

Nutritional value:
- Calories: 180 kcal
- Fat: 12g
- Carbohydrates: 8g
- Fiber: 2g
- Protein: 10g

Directions

1. Preheat the oven to 375°F (190°C). Grease a baking sheet with olive oil.

2. Place the portobello mushrooms, gill side up, on the prepared baking sheet.

3. In a large pan, heat olive oil over medium heat. Add the finely chopped onion and simmer until transparent, approximately 5 minutes.

4. Add minced garlic to the pan and sauté for an additional minute until fragrant.

5. Add fresh spinach leaves to the pan and simmer, turning periodically, until wilted.

6. Remove the pan from heat and toss in crumbled feta cheese and grated Parmesan cheese. Season with salt and pepper, to taste.

7. Spoon the spinach and cheese mixture equally into the cavity of each portobello mushroom.

8. Bake in the preheated oven for 20–25 minutes, or until the mushrooms are soft and the filling is golden brown.

9. Remove the filled mushrooms from the oven and allow them to cool slightly before serving.

10. Garnish with fresh parsley before serving.

QUICK TIPS

You may add chopped sun-dried tomatoes or pine nuts to the spinach and cheese combination for extra flavor and texture. Serve the filled portobello mushrooms as a main meal or with a salad or roasted vegetables.

4 MEDITERRANEAN RATATOUILLE

Prep Time: 20 minutes Cooking Time: 40 minutes Total Time: 1 hour Servings: 6

Ingredients

- 2 tablespoons olive oil;
- 1 onion, chopped
- 2 cloves garlic, minced
- 1 eggplant, diced; 1 zucchini, diced;
- 1 yellow squash, diced; 1 red bell pepper, diced;
- 1 yellow bell pepper, diced;
- 1 can (14.5 ounces) of diced tomatoes
- 2 tablespoons tomato paste;
- 1 teaspoon dried thyme;
- 1 teaspoon dried oregano; salt and pepper to taste;
- fresh basil leaves for garnish

Nutritional value:
- Calories: 120 kcal
- Fat: 5g
- Carbohydrates: 18g
- Fiber: 6g
- Protein: 4g

Directions

1. Heat olive oil in a large pan or Dutch oven over medium heat. Add chopped onion and sauté until translucent, approximately 5 minutes.

2. Add minced garlic to the pan and sauté for an additional minute until fragrant.

3. Add diced eggplant, diced zucchini, diced yellow squash, diced red bell pepper, and diced yellow bell pepper to the skillet. Cook, stirring periodically, for 10–15 minutes until veggies are softened.

4. Stir in diced tomatoes (with their liquids), tomato paste, dry thyme, dried oregano, salt, and pepper. Bring the mixture to a simmer.

5. Reduce the heat to low and allow the ratatouille to simmer uncovered for 15-20 minutes, stirring periodically, until the flavors have merged and the veggies are soft.

6. Taste and adjust seasoning as required.

7. Remove the ratatouille from the heat and allow it to cool slightly before serving.

8. Garnish with fresh basil leaves before serving

QUICK TIPS

Ratatouille may be served warm or at room temperature. It's delicious on its own as a vegetarian main meal, or served over grilled chicken, fish, or crusty bread. Leftover ratatouille may be kept in an airtight jar in the refrigerator for up to 3 days.

5 MEDITERRANEAN STUFFED GRAPE LEAVES (DOLMAS)

Prep Time: 30 minutes Cooking Time: 1 hour Total Time: 1 hour 30 minutes Servings: 6

Ingredients

- 1 jar (16 ounces) of grape leaves in brine, drained, and rinsed
- 1 cup cooked rice (such as long-grain white rice or brown rice)
- 1/2 cup cooked lentils; 1/4 cup chopped fresh parsley;
- 1/4 cup chopped fresh dill;
- 1/4 cup chopped fresh mint 1/4 cup chopped green onions
- 1/4 cup pine nuts; 2 tablespoons olive oil Juice of 1 lemon
- Salt and pepper to taste; Greek yogurt for serving (optional)

Nutritional value:

- Calories: 180 kcal
- Fat: 10g
- Carbohydrates: 20g
- Fiber: 3g
- Protein: 4g

Directions

1. In a large mixing bowl, add cooked rice, cooked lentils, chopped fresh parsley, chopped fresh dill, chopped fresh mint, chopped green onions, pine nuts, olive oil, lemon juice, salt, and pepper. Mix until completely blended.

2. On a clean work surface, lay a grape leaf flat, shining side down. Place a spoonful of the rice and lentil mixture at the grape leaf's stem end.

3. Fold the grape leaf's bottom over the filling, then fold in the sides and roll it tightly into a cylinder.

4. Repeat with the remaining grape leaves and filling.

5. Arrange the packed grape leaves in a big pot in a single layer, seam side down.

6. Pour enough water over the filled grape leaves to cover them by 1 inch.

7. Place a heatproof plate or cover directly on

QUICK TIPS

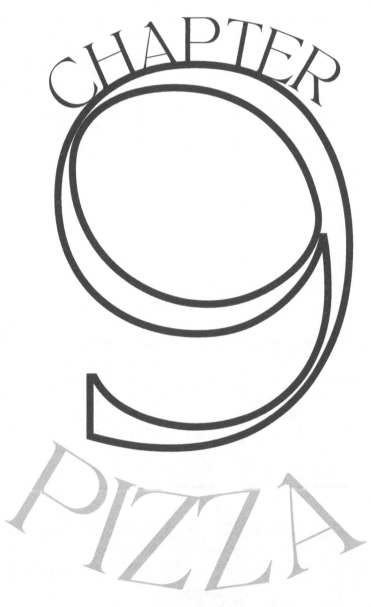

CHAPTER

9

PIZZA

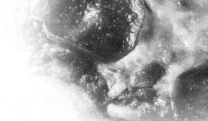

1 MEDITERRANEAN VEGGIE PIZZA

Prep Time: 20 minutes Cooking Time: 15 minutes Total Time:35 minutes Servings: 4

Ingredients

- 1 pre-made whole wheat pizza dough; 1/2 cup marinara sauce
- 1 cup shredded mozzarella cheese 1/2 cup sliced cherry tomatoes
- 1/4 cup sliced black olives
- 1/4 cup chopped red onion
- 1/4 cup sliced bell peppers (any color)
- 1/4 cup crumbled feta cheese
- Fresh basil leaves for garnish;
- olive oil for drizzling; salt and pepper to taste

Nutritional value:
- Calories: 280 kcal
- Fat: 10g
- Carbohydrates: 35g
- Fiber: 5g
- Protein: 12g

Directions

1. Preheat the oven to 425°F (220°C). Place the pizza dough on a lightly floured board and roll it out into a circle.

2. Transfer the rolled-out dough to a pizza stone or baking sheet.

3. Spread marinara sauce evenly over the pizza crust, leaving a little border around the edges.

4. Sprinkle shredded mozzarella cheese over the sauce.

5. Arrange sliced cherry tomatoes, black olives, red onion, and bell peppers on top of the cheese.

6. Crumble feta cheese over the veggies.

7. Season the pizza to taste with salt and pepper.

8. Drizzle olive oil over top of the pizza.

9. Bake in the preheated oven for 12–15 minutes, or until the crust is golden brown and the cheese is bubbling and melted.

10. Remove the pizza from the oven and allow it to cool slightly before slicing.

11. Garnish with fresh basil leaves before serving.

QUICK TIPS

You may change the toppings according to your desire. Feel free to add additional Mediterranean ingredients, such as artichoke hearts, sun-dried tomatoes, or roasted garlic.
For a crispy crust, preheat your pizza stone in the oven before putting the rolled-out dough on it.

2 MEDITERRANEAN CHICKEN PESTO PIZZA

Prep Time: 25 minutes Cooking Time: 15 minutes Total Time: 40 minutes Servings: 4

Ingredients

- 1 pre-made whole wheat pizza dough;
- 1/2 cup basil pesto;
- 1 cup cooked and shredded chicken breast
- 1/2 cup sliced cherry tomatoes
- 1/4 cup sliced black olives
- 1/4 cup sliced red onion
- 1/4 cup crumbled feta cheese
- 1/4 cup shredded mozzarella cheese
- Fresh basil leaves for garnish; olive oil for drizzling; salt and pepper to taste

Nutritional value:
- Calories: 320 kcal
- Fat: 14g
- Carbohydrates: 30g
- Fiber: 3g;
- Protein: 20g

Directions

1. Preheat the oven to 425°F (220°C). Place the pizza dough on a lightly floured board and roll it out into a circle.

2. Transfer the rolled-out dough to a pizza stone or baking sheet.

3. Spread basil pesto evenly over the pizza dough, leaving a little border around the edges.

4. Sprinkle cooked and shredded chicken breast over the pesto.

5. Arrange sliced cherry tomatoes, black olives, and red onion on top of the chicken.

6. Sprinkle crumbled feta cheese and shredded mozzarella cheese over the toppings.

7. Season the pizza to taste with salt and pepper.

8. Drizzle olive oil over top of the pizza.

9. Bake in the preheated oven for 12–15 minutes, or until the crust is golden brown and the cheese is bubbling and melted.

10. Remove the pizza from the oven and allow it to cool slightly before slicing.

11. Garnish with fresh basil leaves before serving.

QUICK TIPS

You may use store-bought basil pesto or prepare your own homemade pesto for an additional fresh taste.
If you want a vegetarian alternative, you may skip the chicken and add extra veggies such as roasted red peppers or artichoke hearts.

3 GREEK-STYLE MEDITERRANEAN PIZZA

Prep Time: 20 minutes Cooking Time: 15 minutes Total Time: 35 minutes Servings: 4

Ingredients

- ·1 pre-made whole wheat pizza dough;
- ·1/2 cup tzatziki sauce
- ·1 cup cooked and diced chicken or gyro meat;
- · 1/4 cup sliced red onion;
- ·1/4 cup sliced black olives
- ·1/4 cup crumbled feta cheese;
- ·1/4 cup diced tomatoes;
- ·1 tablespoon chopped fresh parsley;
- ·olive oil for drizzling; salt and pepper to taste

Nutritional value:
- Calories: 290 kcal
- Fat: 12g
- Carbohydrates: 30g
- Fiber: 3g
- Protein: 15g

Directions

1. Preheat the oven to 425°F (220°C). Place the pizza dough on a lightly floured board and roll it out into a circle.

2. Transfer the rolled-out dough to a pizza stone or baking sheet.

3. Spread tzatziki sauce evenly over the pizza crust, leaving a little boundary around the borders.

4. Sprinkle cooked and diced chicken or gyro meat over the tzatziki sauce.

5. Arrange sliced red onion, black olives, and chopped tomatoes on top of the chicken.

6. Sprinkle crumbled feta cheese over the toppings.

7. Season the pizza to taste with salt and pepper.

8. Drizzle olive oil over top of the pizza.

9. Bake in the preheated oven for 12–15 minutes, or until the crust is golden brown and the cheese is bubbling and melted.

10. Remove the pizza from the oven and allow it to cool slightly before slicing.

11. Garnish with chopped fresh parsley before serving.

QUICK TIPS

Tzatziki sauce gives a refreshing and tangy taste to the pizza. You can get it in the refrigerated department of most grocery shops, or you can make your own at home. - Serve this Greek-style pizza with a side salad of mixed greens seasoned with lemon juice and olive oil for a full Mediterranean supper

3 MEDITERRANEAN FLATBREAD PIZZA

Prep Time: 15 minutes Cooking Time: 10 minutes Total Time: 25 minutes Servings: 2

Ingredients

- 2 whole wheat flatbreads or naan loaves
- 1/2 cup hummus 1/2 cup roasted red peppers, sliced
- 1/4 cup sliced black olives
- 1/4 cup crumbled feta cheese; 2 tablespoons chopped fresh parsley; olive oil for drizzling; salt and pepper to taste.

Nutritional value:
- Calories: 250 kcal
- Fat: 10g
- Carbohydrates: 30g
- Fiber: 3g
- Protein: 10g

Directions

1. Preheat the oven to 400°F (200°C). Place the flatbreads or naan breads on a baking pan.

2. Spread hummus equally over each flatbread, leaving a little border around the borders.

3. Arrange sliced roasted red peppers and black olives on top of the hummus.

4. Sprinkle crumbled feta cheese over the toppings.

5. To taste, season the flatbreads with salt and pepper.

6. Drizzle olive oil over top of each flatbread.

7. Bake in the preheated oven for 8–10 minutes, or until the edges are crispy and the toppings are cooked through.

8. Remove the flatbreads from the oven and allow them to cool slightly before slicing.

9. Garnish with chopped fresh parsley before serving.

QUICK TIPS

You may modify the toppings by adding items like artichoke hearts, sun-dried tomatoes, or grilled vegetables. This flatbread pizza is a fast and simple weekday supper. For a balanced supper, serve it with a side salad of mixed greens dressed with balsamic vinaigrette.

4 MEDITERRANEAN PITA PIZZA

Prep Time: 15 minutes Cooking Time: 10 minutes Total Time:25 minutes Servings: 2

Ingredients

- 2 whole wheat pitas 1/2 cup marinara sauce
- 1/2 cup chopped cherry tomatoes
- 1/4 cup sliced black olives
- 1/4 cup crumbled feta cheese;
- 2 tablespoons chopped fresh basil;
- olive oil for drizzling;
- Salt and pepper to taste.

Nutritional value:

- Calories: 230 kcal
- Fat: 8g
- Carbohydrates: 30g
- Fiber: 3g
- Protein: 10g

Directions

1. Preheat the oven to 400°F (200°C). Place the pitas on a baking sheet.

2. Spread marinara sauce equally over each pita, leaving a little border around the borders.

3. Arrange sliced cherry tomatoes and black olives on top of the sauce.

4. Sprinkle crumbled feta cheese over the toppings.

5. To taste, season the pitas with salt and pepper.

6. Drizzle olive oil on top of each pita.

7. Bake in the preheated oven for 8–10 minutes, or until the edges are crispy and the toppings are cooked through.

8. Remove the pitas from the oven and allow them to cool slightly before slicing.

9. Garnish with chopped fresh basil before serving.

QUICK TIPS

You may add cooked chicken, shrimp, or tofu for added protein.
Pita pizzas are perfect for individual servings and may be personalized with your favorite Mediterranean toppings.
Experiment with a variety of combinations to discover your fave!

CHAPTER 10

FISH & SEAFOOD

1 MEDITERRANEAN GRILLED SALMON

Prep Time: 10 minutes Marinating Time: 30 minutes Cooking Time: 10 minutes Total Time: 50 minutes Servings: 4

Ingredients

- 4 salmon fillets (approximately 6 ounces each), skin-on;
- 1/4 cup olive oil; 2 teaspoons lemon juice
- 2 cloves garlic, minced
- 1 teaspoon dried oregano; 1 teaspoon dry thyme;
- 1 teaspoon smoked paprika
- Salt and pepper to taste;
- Lemon wedges; and fresh parsley for garnish.

Nutritional value:

- Calories: 250 kcal
- Fat: 15g
- Carbohydrates: 2g
- Protein: 25g

Directions

1. In a small bowl, mix together olive oil, lemon juice, minced garlic, dried oregano, dried thyme, smoked paprika, salt, and pepper to form the marinade.

2. Place the salmon fillets in a shallow dish or resealable plastic bag. Pour the marinade over the salmon, ensuring that each fillet is uniformly covered. Cover or refrigerate for at least 30 minutes to marinate.

3. Preheat the grill to medium-high heat. Oil the grill grates to avoid sticking.

4. Remove the salmon fillets from the marinade, brushing off any excess marinade. Discard the leftover marinade.

5. Place the salmon fillets on the prepared grill, skin-side down. Grill for 4-5 minutes on each side, or until the salmon is cooked through and flakes readily with a fork.

6. Once done, take the salmon from the grill and transfer it to a serving plate.

7. Garnish with lemon wedges and fresh parsley before serving.

QUICK TIPS

Serve grilled salmon with a side of roasted vegetables or a mixed green salad drizzled with olive oil and balsamic vinegar for a balanced dinner.
Be mindful not to overcook the salmon to ensure it remains juicy and tasty.

2 MEDITERRANEAN SHRIMP SCAMPI

Prep Time: 15 minutes Cooking Time: 10 minutes Total Time: 25 minutes Servings: 4

Ingredients

- 1 pound of big shrimp, peeled and deveined;
- 4 tablespoons of olive oil 4 cloves garlic, minced
- 1/4 teaspoon red pepper flakes (adjust to taste)
- zest and juice of 1 lemon
- 1/4 cup dry white wine (optional)
- 1/4 cup chopped fresh parsley
- Salt and pepper to taste; cooked whole wheat spaghetti or linguine for dishing (optional)
- grated Parmesan cheese for serving (optional)

Nutritional value:
- Calories: 200 kcal
- Fat: 10g
- Carbohydrates: 5g
- Protein: 20g

Directions

1. Heat 2 tablespoons of olive oil in a large pan over medium heat. Add minced garlic and red pepper flakes, and sauté for 1-2 minutes until aromatic.

2. Add the shrimp to the skillet in a single layer. Cook for 2-3 minutes, then turn the shrimp and cook for a further 2-3 minutes until pink and cooked through.

3. Remove the shrimp from the pan and transfer them to a platter. Cover to stay warm.

4. In the same skillet, add the remaining 2 tablespoons of olive oil, lemon zest, lemon juice, and white wine (if using). Cook for 2-3 minutes, scraping up any browned pieces from the bottom of the pan.

5. Return the cooked shrimp to the skillet. Toss to coat the shrimp in the sauce, then cook for a further minute to heat through.

6. Stir in chopped fresh parsley, then season with salt and pepper to taste.

7. Serve the shrimp scampi immediately, either on its own or over cooked whole wheat spaghetti or linguine.

8. Optionally, sprinkle with grated Parmesan cheese before serving.

QUICK TIPS

For a heartier supper, serve Mediterranean shrimp scampi over whole wheat spaghetti or with crusty bread for soaking up the delectable sauce. Feel free to personalize the recipe by adding other veggies, such as cherry tomatoes or spinach, for more taste and nutrients.

3 MEDITERRANEAN BAKED COD WITH TOMATOES & OLIVES

Prep Time:15 minutes Cooking Time: 20 minutes Total Time: 35 minutes Servings: 4

Ingredients

- 4 fish fillets (approximately 6 ounces each)
- 2 cups cherry tomatoes, halved 1/4 cup Kalamata olives, pitted and halved
- 2 cloves garlic, minced
- 2 tablespoons olive oil,
- 1 tablespoon balsamic vinegar, and
- 1 teaspoon dried oregano
- Salt and pepper to taste; fresh basil leaves for garnish

Nutritional value:
- Calories: 180 kcal
- Fat: 8g
- Carbohydrates: 6g
- Protein: 22g

Directions

1. Preheat the oven to 400°F (200°C). Grease a baking dish with olive oil.

2. Place the fish fillets in the prepared baking dish.

3. In a small bowl, add cherry tomatoes, Kalamata olives, minced garlic, olive oil, balsamic vinegar, dried oregano, salt, and pepper. Toss to coat the tomatoes and olives evenly.

4. Spoon the tomato and olive mixture over the fish fillets, spreading everything evenly.

5. Bake in the preheated oven for 15-20 minutes, or until the fish is cooked through and flakes readily with a fork.

6. Remove the roasted fish from the oven and allow it to cool slightly before serving.

7. Garnish with fresh basil leaves before serving.

QUICK TIPS

You may use other white fish, such as halibut or haddock, instead of cod if desired.
Serve baked fish with a side of quinoa, couscous, or roasted veggies for a full supper.

4 MEDITERRANEAN GARLIC SHRIMP PASTA

Prep Time: 15 minutes Cooking Time: 15 minutes Total Time: 30 minutes Servings: 4

Ingredients

- 8 ounces of whole wheat spaghetti or linguine
- 1 pound of large, peeled and deveined shrimp;
- 4 tablespoons of olive oil 4 cloves garlic, minced
- 1/4 teaspoon red pepper flakes (adjust to taste)
- 1/4 cup chopped fresh parsley; zest and juice of 1 lemon
- Salt and pepper to taste grated Parmesan cheese for serving (optional)

Nutritional value:
- Calories: 320 kcal
- Fat: 12g
- Carbohydrates: 40g
- Protein: 16g

Directions

1. Cook the pasta according to package directions until al dente. Drain and put aside.

2. Meanwhile, heat 2 tablespoons of olive oil in a large pan over medium heat. Add minced garlic and red pepper flakes, and sauté for 1-2 minutes until aromatic.

3. Add the shrimp to the skillet in a single layer. Cook for 2-3 minutes, then turn the shrimp and cook for a further 2-3 minutes until pink and cooked through.

4. Remove the shrimp from the pan and transfer them to a platter. Cover to stay warm.

5. In the same skillet, add the remaining 2 tablespoons of olive oil. Return the cooked pasta to the skillet. Toss to coat the spaghetti in garlic-infused olive oil.

6. Add chopped fresh parsley, lemon zest, and lemon juice to the skillet. Toss to blend.

7. Return the cooked shrimp to the skillet. Toss to coat the shrimp in the spaghetti, and reheat through.

8. Season to taste with salt and pepper.

9. Serve the garlic shrimp pasta immediately, perhaps topped with grated Parmesan cheese.

QUICK TIPS

For a richer sauce, you may add a splash of white wine or chicken stock to the pan before adding the pasta. Feel free to add more veggies, such as cherry tomatoes, spinach, or roasted red peppers, for more taste and color.

5 MEDITERRANEAN GRILLED SWORDFISH WITH LEMON HERB SAUCE

Prep Time: 15 minutes Marinating Time: 30 minutes Cooking Time: 10 minutes Total Time: 55 minutes Servings: 4

Ingredients

- 4 swordfish steaks (approximately 6 ounces each)
- 1/4 cup olive oil; 2 teaspoons lemon juice
- 2 cloves garlic, minced
- 1 teaspoon dried oregano
- 1 teaspoon dried thyme; salt and pepper to taste;
- fresh parsley for garnish

LEMON HERB SAUCE:
- 1/4 cup olive oil; zest and juice of 1 lemon
- 2 tablespoons chopped fresh parsley;
- 1 tablespoon chopped fresh basil 1 clove garlic, minced
- To taste, add salt and pepper.

Nutritional value:
- Calories: 220 kcal
- Fat: 10g
- Carbohydrates: 2g
- Protein: 30g

Directions

1. In a small bowl, mix together olive oil, lemon juice, minced garlic, dried oregano, dried thyme, salt, and pepper to form the marinade.

2. Place the swordfish steaks in a shallow dish or resealable plastic bag. Pour the marinade over the swordfish, ensuring that each steak is uniformly covered. Cover or refrigerate for at least 30 minutes to marinate.

3. Meanwhile, make the lemon herb sauce. In a small bowl, mix together olive oil, lemon zest, lemon juice, chopped fresh parsley, chopped fresh basil, minced garlic, salt, and pepper. Set aside.

4. Preheat the grill to medium-high heat. Oil the grill grates to avoid sticking.

5. Remove the swordfish steaks from the marinade, brushing off any excess marinade. Discard the leftover marinade.

6. Place the swordfish steaks on the prepared grill. Grill for 4-5 minutes on each side, or until the swordfish is cooked through and flakes readily with a fork.

7. Once done, take the swordfish steaks from the grill and transfer them to a serving plate.

8. Drizzle the lemon herb sauce over the cooked swordfish steaks.

9. Garnish with fresh parsley before serving.

QUICK TIPS

Serve grilled swordfish with your favorite Mediterranean side dishes such as roasted vegetables, couscous, or a Greek salad.
Be mindful not to overcook the swordfish to ensure it remains juicy and tasty.

CHAPTER
11

BEEF PORK & LAMB

1 MEDITERRANEAN LAMB KEBABS

Prep Time: 20 minutes Marinating Time: 1 hour Cooking Time: 10 minutes Total Time: 1 hour 30 minutes Servings: 4

Ingredients

- 1 pound lamb leg or shoulder, cut into 1-inch cubes
- 1/4 cup olive oil;
- 2 teaspoons lemon juice
- 2 cloves garlic, minced
- 1 teaspoon dried oregano
- 1 teaspoon dried thyme;
- 1 teaspoon smoked paprika
- Salt and pepper to taste wooden skewers, soaking in water for 30 minutes

Nutritional value:
- Calories: 280 kcal
- Fat: 15g
- Carbohydrates: 5g
- Protein: 30g

Directions

1. In a large mixing bowl, whisk together olive oil, lemon juice, minced garlic, dried oregano, dried thyme, smoked paprika, salt, and pepper to form the marinade.

2. Add the cubed lamb to the marinade, ensuring that each piece is equally covered. Cover the bowl and refrigerate for at least 1 hour to marinate.

3. Preheat the grill to medium-high heat.

4. Thread the marinated lamb cubes onto the moistened wooden skewers, allowing a little space between each piece.

5. Grill the lamb kebabs for 4-5 minutes on each side, or until they are cooked to your preferred doneness and have excellent grill marks.

6. Once done, take the lamb kebabs from the grill and allow them to rest for a few minutes before serving.

7. Serve the lamb kebabs with your choice of side dishes, such as rice pilaf, grilled vegetables, or a Greek salad.

QUICK TIPS

For added flavor, you may add bits of bell peppers, onions, and cherry tomatoes to the skewers along with the lamb. Make sure to soak the wooden skewers in water for at least 30 minutes before grilling to prevent them from burning.

2 MEDITERRANEAN PORK SOUVLAKI WITH TZATZIKI SAUCE

Prep Time: 20 minutes Marinating Time: 2 hours Cooking Time: 15 minutes Total Time: 2 hours 35 minutes Servings: 4

Ingredients

- 1 pound of pork tenderloin, sliced into 1-inch cubes
- 1/4 cup olive oil;
- 2 teaspoons lemon juice
- 2 cloves garlic, minced
- 1 teaspoon dried oregano
- 1 teaspoon dried thyme
- Salt and pepper to taste wooden skewers, soaking in water for 30 minutes

TZATZIKI SAUCE:
- 1 cup Greek yogurt
- 1/2 cucumber, grated and pressed to remove extra moisture
- 1 clove garlic, minced
- 1 tablespoon of lemon juice
- 1 tablespoon chopped fresh dill;
- salt and pepper to taste

Nutritional value:
- Calories: 320 kcal
- Fat: 20g
- Carbohydrates: 10g
- Protein: 25g

Directions

1. In a large mixing bowl, whisk together olive oil, lemon juice, minced garlic, dried oregano, dried thyme, salt, and pepper to form the marinade.

2. Add the cubed pork to the marinade, ensuring that each piece is well covered. Cover the bowl and refrigerate for at least 2 hours to marinate.

3. While the pork is marinating, make the tzatziki sauce. In a small bowl, add Greek yogurt, grated cucumber, minced garlic, lemon juice, chopped fresh dill, salt, and pepper. Mix thoroughly and chill until ready to serve.

4. Preheat the grill to medium-high heat.

5. Thread the marinated pork cubes onto the moistened wooden skewers, allowing a little space between each piece.

6. Grill the pork souvlaki for 5–6 minutes on each side, or until they are cooked through and have excellent grill marks.

7. Once done, take the pork souvlaki from the grill and let it rest for a few minutes before serving.

8. On the side, serve the pork souvlaki with tzatziki sauce, pita bread, and your choice of Mediterranean sides.

QUICK TIPS

For a full dinner, serve pig souvlaki with warm pita bread, tzatziki sauce, and a Greek salad. If using wooden skewers, ensure to soak them in water for at least 30 minutes before grilling to prevent them from burning.

3 MEDITERRANEAN BEEF SKEWERS WITH CHIMICHURRI SAUCE

Prep Time: 20 minutes Marinating Time: 2 hours Cooking Time: 10 minutes Total Time: 2 hours 30 minutes Servings: 4

Ingredients

- 1 pound of beef sirloin or tenderloin, cut into 1-inch chunks
- 1/4 cup olive oil
- 2 teaspoons of red wine vinegar
- 2 cloves garlic, minced
- 1 teaspoon dried oregano
- 1 teaspoon smoked paprika
- To taste, add salt and pepper. wooden skewers, soaking in water for 30 minutes

CHIMICHURRI SAUCE:

- 1 cup fresh parsley leaves, finely chopped
- 1/4 cup fresh cilantro leaves, finely chopped 2 cloves garlic, minced
- 1/4 cup red wine vinegar
- 1/2 cup olive oil
- 1/2 teaspoon red pepper flakes
- To taste, add salt and pepper.

Nutritional value:
- Calories: 320 kcal
- Fat: 18g
- Carbohydrates: 5g
- Protein: 35g

Directions

1. In a large mixing basin, whisk together olive oil, red wine vinegar, minced garlic, dried oregano, smoked paprika, salt, and pepper to form the marinade.

2. Add the cubed meat to the marinade, ensuring that each piece is well covered. Cover the bowl and refrigerate for at least 2 hours to marinate.

3. While the steak is marinating, create the chimichurri sauce. In a small bowl, add chopped parsley, chopped cilantro, minced garlic, red wine vinegar, olive oil, red pepper flakes, salt, and pepper. Mix thoroughly and set aside.

4. Preheat the grill to medium-high heat.

5. Thread the marinated beef cubes onto the moistened wooden skewers, allowing a little space between each piece.

6. Grill the beef skewers for 3–4 minutes on each side, or until they are cooked to your preferred doneness and have excellent grill marks.

7. Once done, take the meat skewers from the grill and allow them to rest for a few minutes before serving.

8. Serve the meat skewers with a side of chimichurri sauce.

QUICK TIPS

Chimichurri sauce may be prepared ahead of time and kept in the refrigerator for up to a week. The tastes will mix together and increase with time.
Serve beef skewers with grilled veggies, roasted potatoes, or a mixed green salad for a full supper.

4 MEDITERRANEAN PORK TENDERLOIN WITH ROASTED VEGETABLES

Prep Time: 15 minutes Marinating Time: 1 hour Cooking Time: 25 minutes Total Time: 1 hour 40 minutes Servings: 4

Ingredients

- 1 pound pork tenderloin;
- 1/4 cup olive oil 2 teaspoons balsamic vinegar;
- 2 cloves garlic, minced
- 1 teaspoon dried rosemary
- 1 teaspoon dried thyme
- To taste, add salt and pepper.

ROASTED VEGETABLES:
- 2 cups mixed veggies (such as bell peppers, zucchini, cherry tomatoes, and red onion), chopped
- 2 tablespoons of olive oil
- To taste, add salt and pepper.

Nutritional value:
- Calories: 280 kcal
- Fat: 12g
- Carbohydrates: 10g
- Protein: 30g

Directions

1. In a large mixing bowl, whisk together olive oil, balsamic vinegar, minced garlic, dried rosemary, dried thyme, salt, and pepper to form the marinade.

2. Place the pork tenderloin in a shallow dish or resealable plastic bag. Pour the marinade over the pork, ensuring it is uniformly covered. Cover or seal and refrigerate for at least 1 hour to marinate.

3. Preheat the oven to 400°F (200°C).

4. In a separate mixing dish, combine the mixed veggies with olive oil, salt, and pepper until covered.

5. Place the marinated pork tenderloin on a baking sheet lined with parchment paper or aluminum foil. Arrange the mixed veggies around the pork.

6. Roast in the preheated oven for 20–25 minutes, or until the pork achieves an internal temperature of 145°F (63°C) and the veggies are cooked, tossing the vegetables halfway through.

7. Once done, remove the pork tenderloin from the oven and let it rest for a few minutes before slicing.

8. Serve the sliced pork tenderloin with the roasted veggies.

QUICK TIPS

Feel free to modify the roasted veggies using your favorite seasonal vegetables or whatever you have on hand. For added flavor, you may coat the pork tenderloin with any residual marinade before roasting.

5 MEDITERRANEAN LAMB MEATBALLS WITH TZATZIKI SAUCE

Prep Time:20 minutes Cooking Time: 20 minutes Total Time: 40 minutes Servings: 4

Ingredients

- 1 pound ground lamb,
- 1/4 cup breadcrumbs
- 1/4 cup grated Parmesan cheese;
- 1/4 cup chopped fresh parsley 1 clove garlic, minced
- 1 teaspoon dried oregano
- 1 teaspoon dried mint
- Salt and pepper to taste; olive oil for cooking

TZATZIKI SAUCE:

- 1 cup Greek yogurt
- 1/2 cucumber, grated and pressed to remove extra moisture
- 1 clove garlic, minced
- 1 tablespoon of lemon juice
- 1 tablespoon chopped fresh dill; salt and pepper to taste

Nutritional value:

- Calories: 280 kcal
- Fat: 15g
- Carbohydrates: 10g
- Protein: 25g

Directions

1. In a large mixing bowl, combine ground lamb, breadcrumbs, grated Parmesan cheese, chopped parsley, minced garlic, dried oregano, dried mint, salt, and pepper. Mix until completely blended.

2. Roll the mixture into golf ball-sized meatballs.

3. Heat olive oil in a large pan over medium heat. Add the meatballs to the skillet in a single layer, ensuring not to overcrowd the pan.

4. Cook the meatballs for 8–10 minutes, flipping regularly, until they are browned on both sides and cooked thoroughly.

5. While the meatballs are cooking, make the tzatziki sauce. In a small bowl, add Greek yogurt, grated cucumber, minced garlic, lemon juice, chopped dill, salt, and pepper. Mix thoroughly and chill until ready to serve.

6. Once cooked, take the meatballs from the pan and drain on paper towels to remove excess oil.

7. Serve the lamb meatballs hot, with the tzatziki sauce on the side.

QUICK TIPS

Feel free to modify the roasted veggies using your favorite seasonal vegetables or whatever you have on hand. For added flavor, you may coat the pork tenderloin with any residual marinade before roasting.

CHAPTER
12

BEANS AND GRAINS

1 MEDITERRANEAN QUINOA SALAD

Prep Time: 15 minutes Cooking Time: 15 minutes Total Time: 30 minutes Servings: 4

Ingredients

- 1 cup quinoa, rinsed;
- 2 cups water or vegetable broth;
- 1 cup cherry tomatoes,
- halved 1 cucumber, diced;
- 1/4 cup Kalamata olives, pitted and halved
- 1/4 cup crumbled feta cheese;
- 1/4 cup chopped fresh parsley;
- 2 tablespoons extra virgin olive oil;
- 2 teaspoons lemon juice
- 1 clove garlic, minced
- 1 teaspoon dried oregano
- To taste, add salt and pepper.

Nutritional value:

- Calories: 280 kcal
- Fat: 10g
- Carbohydrates: 35g
- Protein: 12g

Directions

1. In a medium saucepan, bring water or vegetable broth to a boil. Add quinoa and lower the heat to low. Cover and boil for 15 minutes, or until quinoa is cooked and water is absorbed. Remove it from the heat and let it cool slightly.

2. In a large mixing bowl, add cooked quinoa, half cherry tomatoes, sliced cucumber, halved Kalamata olives, crumbled feta cheese, and chopped fresh parsley.

3. In a separate bowl, mix together extra virgin olive oil, lemon juice, minced garlic, dried oregano, salt, and pepper to prepare the dressing.

4. Pour the dressing over the quinoa salad and toss until evenly covered.

5. Taste and adjust seasoning as required.

6. Serve the Mediterranean quinoa salad refrigerated or at room temperature.

QUICK TIPS

You may modify this salad by adding extra veggies such as bell peppers, red onion, or spinach. For additional protein, you may throw in some cooked chickpeas or grilled chicken.

2 MEDITERRANEAN LENTIL SOUP

Prep Time: 15 minutes Cooking Time: 45 minutes Total Time: 1 hour Servings: 6

Ingredients

- 1 cup dry green lentils, washed and drained
- 1 onion, diced; 2 carrots, diced;
- 2 celery stalks, diced; 3 cloves of garlic, minced
- 1 can (14 oz) chopped tomatoes
- 6 cups vegetable broth;
- 1 teaspoon dried oregano;
- 1 teaspoon dried thyme;
- 1 bay leaf; salt and
- Pepper to taste; 2 tablespoons olive oil; and
- 2 tablespoons chopped fresh parsley (for garnish).
- Lemon wedges (for serving)

Nutritional value:
- Calories: 220 kcal
- Fat: 5g
- Carbohydrates: 30g
- Protein: 12g

Directions

1. Heat olive oil in a big saucepan over medium heat. Add chopped onion, carrots, and celery. Cook, stirring occasionally, for 5-7 minutes until veggies are softened.

2. Add minced garlic, dried oregano, and dried thyme. Cook for a further 1-2 minutes until fragrant.

3. Add dry lentils, chopped tomatoes (with their juices), vegetable broth, and bay leaf to the saucepan. Season with salt and pepper, to taste.

4. Bring the soup to a boil, then decrease the heat to low. Cover and boil for 30–40 minutes, or until the lentils are cooked.

5. Once the lentils have cooked, remove the bay leaf from the broth. Taste and adjust seasoning as required.

6. Ladle the Mediterranean lentil soup into dishes and top with chopped fresh parsley.

7. Serve hot, with lemon wedges on the side for squeezing over the soup.

QUICK TIPS

For a heartier soup, you may add diced potatoes or chopped spinach. This soup tastes even better the second day, when the flavors have time to mingle together.

3 MEDITERRANEAN CHICKPEA SALAD

Prep Time: 15 minutes Cooking Time: 0 minutes Total Time: 15 minutes Servings: 4

Ingredients

- 2 cans (15 oz each) of chickpeas, drained and rinsed
- 1 cucumber, diced;
- 1 bell pepper (any color), diced;
- 1/4 cup red onion, finely chopped;
- 1/4 cup Kalamata olives, pitted and halved;
- 1/4 cup crumbled feta cheese;
- 2 tablespoons chopped fresh parsley;
- 2 tablespoons extra virgin olive oil;
- 2 tablespoons lemon juice 1 teaspoon dried oregano
- To taste, add salt and pepper.

Nutritional value:
- Calories: 250 kcal
- Fat: 10g
- Carbohydrates: 30g
- Protein: 10g

Directions

1. In a large mixing bowl, add chickpeas, diced cucumber, diced bell pepper, chopped red onion, halved Kalamata olives, crumbled feta cheese, and chopped fresh parsley.

2. In a separate bowl, mix together extra virgin olive oil, lemon juice, dried oregano, salt, and pepper to prepare the dressing.

3. Pour the dressing over the chickpea salad and toss until evenly covered.
4. Taste and adjust seasoning if required.
5. Serve the Mediterranean chickpea salad refrigerated or at room temperature.

QUICK TIPS

You may modify this salad by adding extra veggies such as cherry tomatoes, chopped avocado, or shredded carrots. For increased nutrition and taste, you may mix in some chopped grilled chicken or cooked quinoa

4 MEDITERRANEAN FARRO SALAD WITH ROASTED VEGETABLES

Prep Time: 15 minutes Cooking Time: 30 minutes Total Time: 45 minutes Servings: 4

Ingredients

- 1 cup farro, washed
- 3 cups water or veggie broth 1 red bell pepper, diced 1 yellow bell pepper, diced
- 1 zucchini, diced
- 1 yellow squash, diced
- 1 red onion, thinly sliced
- 2 tablespoons olive oil;
- 2 tablespoons balsamic vinegar;
- 1 teaspoon dried thyme; salt and pepper to taste;
- 1/4 cup chopped fresh basil (for garnish)

Nutritional value:
- Calories: 280 kcal
- Fat: 8g
- Carbohydrates: 45g
- Protein: 8g

Directions

1. Preheat the oven to 400°F (200°C). Line a baking sheet with parchment paper.

2. In a medium saucepan, bring water or vegetable broth to a boil. Add farro and decrease the heat to low. Cover and simmer for 25–30 minutes, or until the farro is soft. Drain any extra liquid and let it cool somewhat.

3. While the farro is cooking, distribute chopped bell peppers, diced zucchini, diced yellow squash, and thinly sliced red onion on the prepared baking sheet. -

- Drizzle with olive oil and balsamic vinegar, then sprinkle with dried thyme, salt, and pepper. Toss until evenly coated.

4. Roast the veggies in the preheated oven for 20–25 minutes, or until they are soft and slightly browned, tossing halfway through.

5. In a large mixing bowl, add cooked farro and roasted veggies. Toss until evenly blended.

6. Taste and adjust seasoning as required.

7. Serve the Mediterranean farro salad topped with chopped fresh basil.

QUICK TIPS

You may add more roasted veggies, such as cherry tomatoes, eggplant, or asparagus, for more taste and color. This salad may be served warm, at room temperature, or refrigerated, making it excellent for picnics, potlucks, or meal prep.

5 MEDITERRANEAN BLACK BEAN STEW

Ingredients

- 2 cans (15 oz each) of black beans, drained and rinsed
- 1 onion, diced
- 2 cloves garlic, minced
- 1 red bell pepper, chopped
- 1 yellow bell pepper, chopped
- 1 can (14 oz) chopped tomatoes
- 2 cups vegetable broth;
- 1 teaspoon ground cumin;
- 1 teaspoon smoked paprika
- Salt and pepper to taste;
- 2 tablespoons chopped fresh cilantro (for garnish)
- Lime wedges (for serving)

Nutritional value:
- Calories: 220 kcal
- Fat: 6g
- Carbohydrates: 35g
- Protein: 10g

Directions

1. Heat olive oil in a big saucepan over medium heat. Add chopped onion and minced garlic. Cook for 5-7 minutes, stirring occasionally, until onions are cooked and transparent.

2. In the saucepan, add diced red bell pepper and diced yellow bell pepper. Cook for a further 3–4 minutes until the peppers are slightly softened.

3. Add drained and rinsed black beans, chopped tomatoes (with their liquids), vegetable broth, ground cumin, smoked paprika, salt, and pepper to the saucepan. Stir to mix.

4. Bring the stew to a boil, then decrease the heat to low. Cover and boil for 20–25 minutes, stirring regularly, to enable the flavors to melt together.

5. Taste and adjust seasoning as required.

6. Serve the Mediterranean black bean stew hot, topped with chopped fresh cilantro and lime wedges on the side for squeezing over the stew.

QUICK TIPS

For extra texture and taste, you may top the black bean stew with cubed avocado, shredded cheese, or a dollop of Greek yogurt. This stew may be served.
On its own as a substantial vegetarian supper, or you may serve it over cooked rice or quinoa for a full meal.

CHAPTER
13

VEGETABLES & SIDE

101

1 MEDITERRANEAN ROASTED VEGETABLES

Prep Time: 15 minutes Cooking Time: 30 minutes Total Time: 45 minutes Servings: 4

Ingredients

- 1 eggplant, cut into cubes 1 zucchini, sliced into rounds
- 1 yellow squash, cut into rounds
- 1 red bell pepper, sliced into strips
- 1 yellow bell pepper, sliced into strips
- 1 red onion, sliced
- 2 tablespoons extra virgin olive oil
- 2 cloves garlic, minced
- 1 teaspoon dried oregano
- 1 teaspoon dried thyme;
- Salt and pepper to taste;
- And fresh parsley for garnish (optional).

Nutritional value:
- Calories: 120 kcal
- Fat: 7g
- Carbohydrates: 15g
- Protein: 2g

Directions

1. Preheat the oven to 400°F (200°C). Line a baking sheet with parchment paper or aluminum foil.

2. In a large mixing bowl, add the eggplant cubes, zucchini rounds, yellow squash rounds, red bell pepper strips, yellow bell pepper strips, and sliced red onion.

3. In a small bowl, mix together the extra virgin olive oil, minced garlic, dried oregano, dried thyme, salt, and pepper.

4. In the mixing basin, pour the olive oil mixture over the vegetables. Toss until the veggies are uniformly covered.

5. Spread the seasoned veggies in a single layer on the prepared baking sheet.

6. Roast in the preheated oven for 25–30 minutes, or until the veggies are soft and caramelized, stirring halfway through.

7. Once done, remove the roasted veggies from the oven and transfer them to a serving dish.

8. Garnish with fresh parsley, if preferred, and serve hot.

QUICK TIPS

Feel free to adapt this dish by adding additional Mediterranean veggies such as cherry tomatoes, asparagus, or artichoke hearts. Leftover roasted veggies may be kept in an airtight jar in the refrigerator for up to 3 days. They are wonderful served cold or warmed.

2 GREEK LEMON POTATOES

Prep Time: 15 minutes Cooking Time: 60 minutes Total Time: 75 minutes Servings: 4

Ingredients

- 4 big potatoes, peeled and cut into wedges
- 1/4 cup extra virgin olive oil; juice of 2 lemons
- 3 cloves garlic, minced
- 1 teaspoon dried oregano
- Salt and pepper to taste; 1/2 cup veggie broth or water
- Fresh parsley for garnish (optional)

Nutritional value:
- Calories: 180 kcal
- Fat: 6g
- Carbohydrates: 30g
- Protein: 3g

Directions

1. Preheat the oven to 400°F (200°C).

2. In a large mixing bowl, add the potato wedges, extra virgin olive oil, lemon juice, chopped garlic, dried oregano, salt, and pepper. Toss until the potatoes are uniformly covered.

3. Transfer the seasoned potatoes to a baking dish or roasting pan, spreading them out in a single layer.

4. Pour the vegetable broth or water into the baking dish, surrounding the potatoes.

5. Cover the baking dish with aluminum foil and bake in the preheated oven for 45 minutes.

6. After 45 minutes, remove the foil and continue roasting the potatoes for a further 15-20 minutes, or until they are golden brown and crispy on the exterior and soft on the inside.

7. Once done, take the Greek lemon potatoes from the oven and transfer them to a serving plate.

8. Garnish with fresh parsley, if preferred, and serve hot.

QUICK TIPS

For added taste, you may sprinkle some crumbled feta cheese or minced fresh dill over the roasted potatoes before serving. Leftover Greek lemon potatoes may be kept in an airtight jar in the refrigerator for up to 3 days. Prior to serving, reheat them in the oven or microwave.

3 MEDITERRANEAN GRILLED VEGETABLES

Prep Time: 15 minutes Cooking Time: 10 minutes Total Time: 25 minutes Servings: 4

Ingredients

- 1 eggplant, cut into rounds 2 zucchinis, chopped into rounds
- 1 red bell pepper, seeded and sliced into strips
- 1 yellow bell pepper, seeded and sliced into strips
- 1 red onion, cut into rounds
- 2 tablespoons extra virgin olive oil
- 2 cloves garlic, minced
- 1 teaspoon dried oregano
- Salt and pepper to taste; lemon wedges for serving (optional)
- Fresh basil or parsley for garnish (optional)

Nutritional value:

- Calories: 90 kcal
- Fat: 6g
- Carbohydrates: 10g
- Protein: 2g

Directions

1. Preheat the grill to medium-high heat.

2. In a large mixing bowl, add the eggplant rounds, zucchini rounds, red bell pepper strips, yellow bell pepper strips, and sliced red onion.

3. In a small bowl, mix together the extra virgin olive oil, minced garlic, dried oregano, salt, and pepper.

4. In the mixing basin, pour the olive oil mixture over the vegetables. Toss until the veggies are uniformly covered.

5. Thread the seasoned veggies onto skewers, alternating between various kinds of vegetables.

6. Grill the veggie skewers for 3–4 minutes on each side, or until they are cooked and slightly browned.

7. Once done, take the veggie skewers from the grill and place them on a serving plate.

8. Garnish with fresh basil or parsley, if preferred, and serve hot with lemon wedges on the side for squeezing over the veggies.

QUICK TIPS

You may adapt this dish by adding different veggies, like cherry tomatoes, mushrooms, or asparagus. If using wooden skewers, ensure to soak them in water for at least 30 minutes before grilling to prevent them from burning

4 MEDITERRANEAN COUSCOUS SALAD

Prep Time: 15 minutes Cooking Time: 10 minutes Total Time: 25 minutes Servings: 4

Ingredients

- 1 cup couscous;
- 1 1/4 cups veggie broth or water
- 1 cucumber, diced 1 pint of cherry tomatoes, halved
- 1/4 cup Kalamata olives, pitted and halved
- 1/4 cup crumbled feta cheese;
- 2 tablespoons minced fresh parsley;
- 2 tablespoons extra virgin
- olive oil; 2 teaspoons lemon juice
- 1 teaspoon dried oregano
- To taste, add salt and pepper.

Nutritional value:
- Calories: 220 kcal
- Fat: 6g
- Carbohydrates: 35g
- Protein: 6g

Directions

1. In a medium saucepan, bring vegetable broth or water to a boil. Add couscous and toss to mix. Remove from heat, cover, and let it settle for 5 minutes.

2. Fluff the cooked couscous with a fork and transfer it to a large mixing bowl.

3. Add sliced cucumber, halved cherry tomatoes, half Kalamata olives, crumbled feta cheese, and chopped fresh parsley to the bowl with the couscous.

4. In a separate bowl, mix together extra virgin olive oil, lemon juice, dried oregano, salt, and pepper to create the dressing.

5. Pour the dressing over the couscous salad and toss until evenly covered.

6. Taste and adjust seasoning as required.

7. Serve the Mediterranean couscous salad refrigerated or at room temperature.

QUICK TIPS

You may add additional ingredients to this salad, such as sliced red onion, chopped bell peppers, or toasted pine nuts, for more flavor and texture. Leftover couscous salad may be kept in an airtight jar in the refrigerator for up to 3 days. It's perfect for packed lunches or fast dinners on the run.

5 GREEK SPANAKORIZO (SPINACH WITH RICE)

Prep Time: 15 minutes Cooking Time: 30 minutes Total Time: 45 minutes Servings: 4

Ingredients

- 1 cup long-grain white rice;
- 2 tablespoons extra virgin olive oil 1 onion, finely chopped;
- 2 cloves of garlic, minced
- 1 pound fresh spinach, chopped
- 1/4 cup chopped fresh dill,
- 1/4 cup chopped fresh parsley, and 1 teaspoon dried oregano
- 1/2 teaspoon ground nutmeg
- 3 cups veggie broth or water
- Salt and pepper to taste; lemon wedges for serving (optional)

Nutritional value:
- Calories: 180 kcal
- Fat: 6g
- Carbohydrates: 30g
- Protein: 5g

Directions

1. Rinse the rice under cold water until the water runs clear. Drain and put aside.
2. In a large skillet or pot, heat the olive oil over medium heat. Add the chopped onion and simmer until softened, approximately 5 minutes.
3. Add the minced garlic to the saucepan and simmer for an additional 1-2 minutes until fragrant.
4. Stir in the chopped spinach and simmer until wilted, approximately 3–4 minutes.
5. Add the washed rice, chopped fresh dill, chopped fresh parsley, dried oregano, powdered nutmeg, vegetable broth or water, salt, and pepper to the saucepan. Stir to mix.
6. Bring the mixture to a boil, then decrease the heat to low. Cover and boil for 20–25 minutes, or until the rice is cooked and the liquid is absorbed.
7. Once cooked, remove the Greek spanakorizo from the fire and allow it to rest, covered, for 5 minutes.
8. Fluff the rice with a fork and serve hot, with lemon wedges on the side for squeezing over the meal.

QUICK TIPS

You may add additional ingredients to this recipe, such as cooked chickpeas, chopped tomatoes, or Bruised feta cheese adds added flavor and protein. Leftover Greek spanakorizo may be kept in an airtight jar in the refrigerator for up to 3 days. Before serving, reheat it in the microwave or on the stovetop.

30DAYS
MEAL PLANS

Creating a 30-day meal plan based on the principles of the Mediterranean diet might be a wonderful way to add variety, balance, and healthy meals to your routine. The Mediterranean diet emphasizes complete, minimally processed foods such as fruits, vegetables, whole grains, legumes, nuts, seeds, fish, and olive oil, while reducing red meat and saturated fats. Below is an elaborate 30-day meal plan tailored to this eating style?

Day 1

Breakfast: Greek yogurt parfait with fresh berries, granola, and a sprinkle of honey.
Lunch: Mediterranean quinoa salad with chickpeas, cucumbers, cherry tomatoes, feta cheese, and lemon-herb vinaigrette.
Dinner: Grilled lemon herb salmon served with roasted veggies (such as bell peppers, zucchini, and eggplant) with a side of whole grain couscous.

Day 2

Breakfast: Mediterranean vegetable frittata prepared with eggs, spinach, tomatoes, bell peppers, and feta cheese.
Lunch: Greek salad with mixed greens, cucumber, red onion, olives, tomatoes, feta cheese, and lemon-oregano vinaigrette. Serve with whole-grain pita bread.
Dinner: lentil and vegetable stew served with a side of crusty whole grain bread for dipping.

Day 3

Breakfast: Whole grain toast topped with mashed avocado, sliced tomatoes, crumbled feta cheese, and a sprinkling of za'atar flavor.

Lunch: Mediterranean chickpea wrap with hummus, shredded carrots, cucumber, mixed greens, and a sprinkle of tahini sauce. Serve with a serving of tabbouleh salad.

Dinner: Baked Mediterranean chicken thighs with a tomato and olive sauce, served with roasted cauliflower and quinoa.

Day 4

Breakfast: Mediterranean-style omelette with sautéed spinach, roasted red peppers, onions, and crumbled goat cheese.

Lunch: Mediterranean tuna salad prepared with canned tuna, mixed greens, cherry tomatoes, cucumber, red onion, Kalamata olives, and a lemon-herb dressing. Serve with whole-grain crackers.

Dinner: Grilled veggie kebabs with marinated tofu or halloumi cheese, served with whole wheat couscous and tzatziki sauce.

Day 5

Breakfast: Smoothie bowl prepared with Greek yogurt, frozen berries, spinach, banana, and a sprinkling of chia seeds.

Lunch: Falafel salad dish with mixed greens, quinoa, falafel balls, cucumber, tomato, red onion, and a creamy tahini dressing.

Dinner: Spaghetti aglio e olio using whole wheat spaghetti, garlic, olive oil, red pepper flakes, and sautéed broccoli. Serve with a serving of mixed green salad.

Day 6

Breakfast: Whole grain overnight oats with almond milk, chia seeds, sliced almonds, fresh berries, and a drizzle of honey.

Lunch: Mediterranean vegetable and bean soup with a side of full-grain bread.

Dinner: Grilled shrimp skewers with a Greek marinade, accompanied with grilled veggies and quinoa pilaf.

Day 7

Breakfast: Whole-grain English muffin topped with scrambled eggs, sliced avocado, and salsa.

Lunch: Caprese salad with sliced tomatoes, fresh mozzarella cheese, basil leaves, olive oil, and balsamic sauce. Serve with whole-grain breadsticks.

Dinner: Ratatouille cooked with eggplant, zucchini, bell peppers, tomatoes, onions, garlic, and herbs. Serve with crusty whole-grain bread.

Day 8

Breakfast: Greek yogurt dish with sliced bananas, walnuts, honey, and a sprinkling of cinnamon.

Lunch: Mediterranean quinoa tabbouleh salad with cherry tomatoes, cucumber, parsley, mint, lemon juice, and olive oil. Serve with whole-grain pita bread.

Dinner: Baked eggplant parmesan with a side of mixed green salad topped with balsamic vinaigrette.

Day 9

Breakfast: Whole grain toast topped with almond butter, sliced strawberries, and a sprinkling of hemp seeds.

Lunch: Mediterranean-style stuffed bell peppers with quinoa, chickpeas, spinach, feta cheese, and spices. Serve with a side of Greek yogurt and tzatziki sauce.

Dinner: Grilled lemon herb chicken breasts with roasted Brussels sprouts and sweet potatoes.

Day 10

Breakfast: Mediterranean-style avocado toast with sliced tomatoes, crumbled feta cheese, and a sprinkle of balsamic glaze.

Lunch: Greek mezze plate with hummus, tzatziki, grilled veggies, olives, and whole grain pita bread.

Dinner: Mediterranean-style baked cod with cherry tomatoes, olives, capers, and herbs. Serve with quinoa pilaf and steaming green beans.

Day 11

Breakfast: Smoothie prepared with Greek yogurt, spinach, pineapple, banana, and coconut water.

Lunch: Greek spinach and feta-filled chicken breasts served with roasted Mediterranean veggies.

Dinner: Mediterranean-style lentil soup with carrots, celery, tomatoes, and spices. Serve with a side of whole-grain bread.

Day 12

Breakfast: Whole grain pancakes topped with Greek yogurt, mixed berries, and a drizzle of maple syrup.

Lunch: a Mediterranean-style tuna salad sandwich on whole grain bread with lettuce, tomato, cucumber, and red onion.

Dinner: Grilled Mediterranean vegetable and halloumi cheese skewers served with couscous and a side of Greek salad.

Day 13

Breakfast: Mediterranean-style scrambled tofu with cherry tomatoes, spinach, red onion, and herbs. Serve with whole-grain bread.

Lunch: Greek-style stuffed peppers with rice, tomatoes, olives, and feta cheese. Serve with a side of Greek salad.

Dinner: Baked falafel served with tzatziki sauce, whole grain pitas, and a side of tabbouleh salad.

Day 14

Breakfast: Yogurt parfait with layers of Greek yogurt, granola, mixed berries, and honey.

Lunch: Mediterranean-style vegetable and chickpea stew served with healthy grain bread.

Dinner: Grilled lemon garlic shrimp served over whole wheat spaghetti with sautéed spinach and cherry tomatoes.

Day 15

Breakfast: Mediterranean-style avocado and egg breakfast sandwich on whole grain English muffins with sliced tomatoes and arugula.

Lunch: Greek-style quinoa salad with cucumber, bell peppers, red onion, Kalamata olives, and a lemon-oregano vinaigrette. Serve with a side of stuffed grape leaves.

Dinner: Baked Mediterranean vegetable lasagna is created with layers of roasted eggplant, zucchini, bell peppers, tomatoes, and ricotta cheese.

Day 16

Breakfast: Whole grain overnight oats with almond milk, sliced almonds, dried figs, and a drizzle of honey.

Lunch: Mediterranean-style falafel wrap with hummus, tabbouleh, cucumber, tomato, and lettuce. Serve with a side of Greek salad.

Dinner: Grilled lemon herb swordfish, paired with quinoa pilaf and grilled asparagus.

Day 17

Breakfast: Greek yogurt smoothie bowl with frozen berries, banana, spinach, and a sprinkling of granola.

Lunch: Mediterranean-style filled grape leaves with a side of Greek salad and tzatziki sauce.

Dinner: One-pan Mediterranean chicken thighs with roasted potatoes, cherry tomatoes, and green beans.

Day 18

Breakfast: Whole grain toast topped with ricotta cheese, sliced peaches, and a drizzle of honey.

Lunch: Greek-style lentil salad with tomatoes, cucumbers, red onion, feta cheese, and a lemon-herb vinaigrette. Serve with a side of whole-grain pita bread.

Dinner: Baked Mediterranean stuffed peppers with a stuffing of quinoa, black beans, corn, tomatoes, and spices. Serve with a side of Greek salad.

Day 19

Breakfast: Mediterranean-style shakshuka with poached eggs in a tomato and vegetable sauce, served with whole grain bread for dipping.

Lunch: Greek-style grilled veggie sandwich with roasted red peppers, zucchini, eggplant, and feta cheese on whole grain bread. Serve with a side of Greek salad.

Dinner:Grilled lemon garlic chicken kebabs served with a Mediterranean couscous salad.

Day 20

Breakfast: Whole grain waffles topped with Greek yogurt, sliced bananas, and a sprinkle of maple syrup.

Lunch: Mediterranean-style pasta salad with whole wheat spaghetti, cherry tomatoes, cucumbers, olives, feta cheese, and lemon-herb vinaigrette. Serve with a side of Greek salad.

Dinner: Baked Greek-style filled tomatoes with a stuffing of rice, pine nuts, raisins, herbs, and spices. Serve with a side of roasted Mediterranean veggies.

Day 21

Breakfast ; Mediterranean-style avocado and tomato toast with a poached egg on top, dusted with feta cheese and fresh herbs.

Lunch: Greek-style filled grape leaves with a side of Greek salad and tzatziki sauce.

Dinner: Grilled Mediterranean vegetable and tofu skewers served with quinoa and a lemon-herb vinaigrette.

Day 22

Breakfast: Whole grain overnight oats with almond milk, sliced almonds, chopped apple, and a drizzle of maple syrup.

Lunch: Mediterranean-style chickpea salad with cucumber, cherry tomatoes, red onion, parsley, and lemon-oregano vinaigrette. Serve with a side of whole-grain pita bread.

Dinner: Baked Mediterranean fish en papillote with tomatoes, olives, capers, and herbs. Serve with roasted veggies and couscous.

Day 23

Breakfast: Greek yogurt smoothie with frozen mixed berries, banana, spinach, and a scoop of protein powder.

Lunch: Greek-style vegetable and bean soup with a side of full-grain bread.

Dinner: One-pan Mediterranean chicken with artichokes, cherry tomatoes, and olives, served with roasted potatoes.

Day 24

Breakfast: Whole-grain toast topped with mashed avocado, smoked salmon, and sliced cucumber.

Lunch: Mediterranean-style quinoa stuffed peppers with a side of Greek salad.

Dinner: Grilled lemon herb shrimp skewers served with a Greek-style couscous salad.

Day 25

Breakfast: Mediterranean-style scrambled eggs with spinach, sun-dried tomatoes, and feta cheese, served with whole grain bread.

Lunch: Greek-style chicken gyro wrap with grilled chicken, tzatziki sauce, lettuce, tomato, and red onion, wrapped in a whole wheat pita. Serve with a serving of tabbouleh salad.

Dinner: Baked eggplant rollatini packed with ricotta cheese and spinach, served with a side of whole wheat spaghetti and marinara sauce.

Day 26

Breakfast: Greek yogurt parfait with layers of Greek yogurt, granola, mixed berries, and a drizzle of honey.

Lunch: Mediterranean-style lentil and vegetable soup with a side of full-grain bread.

Dinner: Grilled Mediterranean vegetable and halloumi cheese salad with a lemon-herb vinaigrette.

Day 27

Breakfast: Whole grain pancakes topped with sliced bananas, walnuts, and a drizzle of maple syrup.

Lunch: Greek-style falafel salad with mixed greens, cucumber, tomato, red onion, feta cheese, and lemon-oregano vinaigrette.

Dinner: Mediterranean-style baked cod with cherry tomatoes, olives, and capers, served with quinoa and steamed broccoli.

Day 28

Breakfast: Mediterranean-style avocado and egg breakfast sandwich on whole grain English muffins with sliced tomatoes and arugula.

Lunch: Greek-style stuffed tomatoes with a stuffing of rice, pine nuts, raisins, and herbs, served with a side of Greek salad.

Dinner: Grilled lemon garlic chicken thighs paired with roasted Mediterranean veggies and couscous.

Day 29

Breakfast: Yogurt smoothie bowl with Greek yogurt, frozen mixed berries, spinach, and a sprinkling of granola.

Lunch: Mediterranean-style chickpea and vegetable stew with a side of full-grain bread.

Dinner: Baked Greek-style stuffed eggplant with a filling of tomatoes, onions, garlic, and herbs, served with quinoa pilaf.

Day 30

Breakfast: Whole grain bread topped with ricotta cheese, sliced peaches, and a drizzle of honey.

Lunch: Greek-style grilled vegetable and halloumi cheese sandwich with roasted red peppers, zucchini, eggplant, and feta cheese on whole grain bread. Serve with a side of Greek salad.

Dinner: Mediterranean-style shrimp and vegetable stir-fry with a lemon-garlic sauce, served over brown rice.

Feel free to mix and combine these meal ideas to fit your taste preferences and nutritional demands. Additionally, don't forget to add nutritious snacks such as nuts, seeds, fruits, and yogurt throughout the day to keep you energetic and satiated. Enjoy your Mediterranean-inspired cuisine!

Index

12. Mediterranean Vegetable and Chickpea Stew

13. Mediterranean Pasta Salad

14. Mediterranean-style Stuffed Grape Leaves

15. Greek-style Stuffed Peppers

DINNER RECIPES

1. Grilled Lemon Herb Salmon

2. Lentil and vegetable stew

3. Baked Mediterranean Chicken Thighs

4. Spaghetti Aglio and Olio

5. Ratatouille

6. Grilled vegetable kebabs

7. Baked Eggplant Parmesan

8. Grilled Shrimp Skewers

9. Mediterranean Chicken with Artichokes

10. Baked Falafel

11. Mediterranean Fish en Papillote 12. One-Pan Mediterranean Chicken

13. Grilled Lemon Garlic Swordfish

14. Mediterranean Baked Cod

15. Baked Eggplant Rollatini

SNACKS AND APPETIZERS

1. Hummus with crudites

2. Greek Yogurt Dip with Pita Chips

3. Mediterranean Bruschetta

4. Greek-style stuffed mushrooms

5. Mediterranean Vegetable Platter

6. Greek Salad Skewers

7. Stuffed Grape Leaves

8. Greek-style Feta and Olive Tapenade

9. Mediterranean Roasted Chickpeas

10. Tzatziki with Fresh Vegetables

DESSERTS

1. Greek Yogurt with Honey and Walnuts
2. Baklava
3. Greek-style yogurt cheesecake
4. Honey and Greek Yogurt Popsicles
5. Greek Yogurt Parfait with Fresh Fruit
6. Salad with Feta and Watermelon
7. Greek-style Orange and Almond Cake
8. Greek-style Yogurt with Poached Fruit
9. Fig and Walnut Greek Yogurt Bowl
10. Greek-style Yogurt Panna Cotta

STEWS AND SOUPS

1. Greek Lentil Soup
2. Mediterranean Vegetable and Bean Soup
3. Mediterranean-style lentil soup
4. Greek-style Tomato and Orzo Soup
5. Moroccan Chickpea Stew
6. Mediterranean Chicken Soup
7. Greek-style Avgolemono Soup
8. Spanish Chickpea and Spinach Stew
9. Minestrone Soup (Italian)
10. Turkish Red Lentil Soup

VEGETARIAN

1. Mediterranean Vegetable Paella
2. Spinach and Feta Phyllo Pie
3. Stuffed Bell Peppers with Quinoa and Chickpeas
4. Eggplant Parmesan
5. Greek-style Stuffed Tomatoes
6. Mediterranean Quinoa Stuffed Peppers
7. Lentil Moussaka

8. Mediterranean Ratatouille
9. Greek-style Spanakopita
10. Mediterranean Vegetable Tart

PIZZA

1. Greek-style veggie pizza
2. Mediterranean Flatbread Pizza
3. Margherita pizza with whole wheat crust
4. A Greek-style Pita Pizza
5. Mediterranean Cauliflower Crust Pizza
6. Mediterranean Veggie Naan Pizza
7. Greek-style Spinach and Feta Pizza
8. Mediterranean Grilled Veggie Pizza
9. Whole wheat Greek-style pizza
10. Mediterranean Eggplant and Goat Cheese Pizza

FISH AND SEAFOOD

1. Grilled Lemon Herb Salmon
2. Baked Mediterranean Fish en Papillote
3. Grilled Shrimp Skewers
4. Grilled Lemon Garlic Swordfish
5. Mediterranean Baked Cod
6. Greek-style Grilled Octopus
7. Lemon Garlic Shrimp Linguine
8. Mediterranean Seafood Paella
9. Greek-style Grilled Calamari
10. Baked Salmon with Greek Marinade

BEEF, PORK, AND LAMB

1. Mediterranean Beef Kebabs
2. Greek-style Lamb Gyros
3. Moroccan Lamb Tagine

4. Greek-style Pork Souvlaki

5. Mediterranean Beef Stew

6. Greek-style lamb moussaka

7. Mediterranean Lamb Meatballs

8. Grilled pork chops with Greek marinade

9. Greek-style Beef Moussaka

10. Lamb Kofta with Tzatziki Sauce

BEANS AND GRAINS

1. Mediterranean Quinoa Salad

2. Greek Lentil Salad

3. Greek-style Chickpea Salad

4. Mediterranean-style stuffed peppers

5. Greek-style Stuffed Tomatoes

6. Greek-style Baked Gigantes Beans

7. Mediterranean-style lentil and vegetable stew

8. Greek-style Quinoa Stuffed Bell Peppers

9. Moroccan Couscous with Chickpeas

10. Greek-style Rice Pilaf

VEGETABLES AND SIDES

1. Greek-style lemon-roasted potatoes

2. Mediterranean Roasted Vegetables

3. Greek-style Grilled Zucchini

4. Lemon, garlic, and green beans

5. Stuffed eggplant, Greek-style

6. Mediterranean Couscous Salad

7. Greek-style Spinach Rice

8. Grilled Mediterranean Asparagus

9. Tomato and cucumber salad

10. Greek-style Roasted Brussels Sprouts

30-DAY MEAL PLAN

Day 1 Breakfast: Greek Yogurt Parfait

2. Day 1 Lunch: Mediterranean Quinoa Salad

3. Day 1 Dinner: Grilled Lemon Herb Salmon

4. Day 2 Breakfasts: Mediterranean Vegetable Frittata

5. Day 2 Lunches: Greek Salad

6. Day 2 Dinners: Lentil and Vegetable Stew

7. Day 3 Breakfasts: Whole Grain Toast with Avocado

8. Day 3 Lunches: Mediterranean Chickpea Wrap

9. Day 3 Dinners: Baked Mediterranean Chicken Thighs

10. Day 4 breakfast: Smoothie bowl with Greek yogurt

11. Day 4 Lunches: Mediterranean Tuna Salad

12. Day 4 Dinners: Grilled Vegetable Kebabs

13. Day 5 Breakfasts: Greek Yogurt Pancakes

14. Day 5 Lunches: Falafel Salad Bowl

15. Day 5 Dinners: Spaghetti Aglio e Olio

16. Day 6 Breakfast: Whole Grain Overnight Oats

17. Day 6 Lunches: Mediterranean Vegetable and Bean Soup

18. Day 6 Dinners: Grilled Lemon Garlic Shrimp

19. Day 7 Breakfasts: Whole Grain Toast with Ricotta

20. Day 7 Lunches: Caprese Salad

21. Day 7 Dinners: Ratatouille

This index gives a complete guide to all the recipes in your cookbook, sorted by meal type, and further subdivided for easier reference. It also contains a 30-day meal plan to help users plan their meals for a month following the Mediterranean diet principles. Adjust the index depending on the recipes contained in your cookbook, and ensure it is presented cleanly and ordered for clarity and simplicity of use.

Dear valued customer,

I hope you are enjoying your freshly acquired book!
I am glad that you chose to invest in my product and I appreciate you for that.

I recognize that your time is precious, and I am grateful for any further time you may be able to take to offer an honest evaluation. I feel that customer input is vital, and your opinions will help me produce an even better product in the future.
It would be very appreciated if you could take a few minutes to provide an honest review of this book. I genuinely respect your views and ideas and would be glad to get your suggestions on how I might improve.

I appreciate your devotion to my product, and I thank you for taking the time to offer an honest review.

Best Regard
Ernest G. Moore

Made in United States
Orlando, FL
30 September 2024

52177830R00070